11-17

DATE

4-2-18

BORN THAT WAY

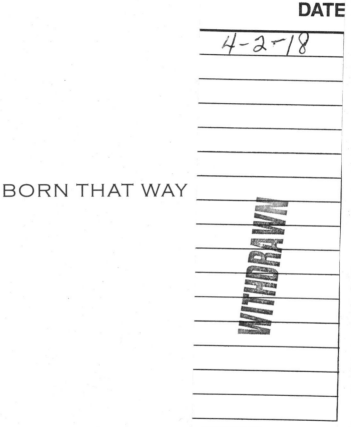

BRODART, CO.

BORN THAT WAY

❄

a novel
by

Susan Ketchen

OOLICHAN BOOKS
LANTZVILLE, BRITISH COLUMBIA, CANADA
2009

Library and Archives Canada Cataloguing in Publication

Ketchen, Susan
Born that way / Susan Ketchen.

ISBN 978-0-88982-254-2

1. Turner's syndrome—Juvenile fiction. I. Title.

PS8621.E893B67 2009   jC813'.6   C2008-907693-1

We gratefully acknowledge the financial support of the Canada
Council for the Arts, the British Columbia Arts Council through
the BC Ministry of Tourism, Small Business and Culture, and the
Government of Canada through the Book Publishing Industry
Development Program, for our publishing activities.

Cover Photo: Isobel Springett

Published by
Oolichan Books
P.O. Box 10, Lantzville
British Columbia, Canada
V0R 2H0

Second printing, November 2009

Printed in Canada

To my family
close and extended
here and gone

And especially to my parents
Doreen and Keith Ketchen
who have been waiting a very long time

CHAPTER ONE

I am galloping flat-out across a field of tall grass on the back of a horse I have never seen before. I am so full of excitement and happiness that my chest could burst. The horse's ears are perked and he requires no urging to keep the pace, and that's just as well because I have no reins, no bridle, no saddle. My fingers clutch deep in a thick wavy mane and I am out of control but at the same time so secure that even if I let go I know I won't fall off. I'll be fine.

We are nearing the end of the field and looming in front of us is a stone wall. Galloping bareback is one thing, jumping is another—but I have no way of stopping. The horse does not slow. He picks his spot and soars above the wall and I fly with him. We land safely on the other side and gallop on along a path snaking through the woods.

There must be a farm ahead—through the trees I hear a ringing sound.

The horse dissolves beneath me.

The alarm clock rings from my bedside table. My fingers clutch my blankets.

I am awake.

Ahead of me is not an unexplored forest, but another day of school. We get our math tests back today. That will be the peak of my excitement.

"I dreamt I was riding again," I tell Mom at breakfast.

"That's nice, Honey." She is eating a piece of dry toast with her tea, and reading.

Because she's not paying attention, I put an extra spoonful of brown sugar on my porridge. Then I say, "I thought we weren't supposed to read magazines at the table."

"This isn't a magazine, Sweetie. It's a new professional journal about my work. See?" She points to the title on the cover and sounds it out, as though the words are too long for me, as though I'm back in elementary school. "*Psychoanalyst Review*," she says.

I'm feeling kind of insulted, even though I know I'm not the world's best speller. But I decide to brush it off with a joke. "Oh, so that's how you spell it," I say. "I always thought you were a Cycle Analyst."

She doesn't laugh, though I hear a snort from Dad. Mom frowns. "There's an article on eating disorders," she says. "And I'm meeting a client this morning who has bulimia. But you're right, Sylvie, I shouldn't be reading at the table. It sets a bad example." She sighs and looks sad. I hate it when she looks sad, but decide against another joke.

"It's okay, Mom. Go ahead—I don't mind."

She pats my hand. "Are you sure?" she asks, but she's reading again before I have a chance to answer.

I add another spoonful of sugar then dribble on the milk. The porridge is a floating island surrounded by a beach of golden brown sand. When I have a horse one day I will canter along a beach like this and plunge in and out of the breaking waves. "I was galloping and we jumped a gigantic stone wall and I stayed on," I say.

"Quiet—the stock market report is on," says Dad, adjusting the volume on the radio. Dad loves hearing the morning market news on the radio even though he's already spent half an hour reading updates on the computer. I listen to the commodities report with him. Mom notices all the extra sugar in my bowl and is about to say something, but Dad shushes her, so she frowns at me and then goes back to her journal.

After breakfast I ride my bike to school. I take the long way around the outer edge of the subdivision and then turn onto Willow Bend Road. I'm not in any sort of hurry to arrive at school. I'm kind of worried about the math test as this is my weakest subject. In everything else I can usually earn B's, but math is something else—I have to work extra hard and even then sometimes I barely pass.

School is harder this year than it was last year, and my math teacher, Mr. Brumby, doesn't like me. Plus, I was popular last year, but that was before The Twins arrived from Manitoba. It's not as though they were from somewhere special like Mars or Vienna, and it's not as though it's such a great accomplishment to be a twin, but everyone treats them as though they're special and now I'm nothing. They're not even identical.

Last year after school Logan Losino asked if there was someone he could beat up for me. Last year there was always someone who wanted to hang out with me. Now there's a line-up to hang out with Amber and Topaz. Logan Losino has a crush on Amber. He punched Jerry Jinzhou for her and she was so happy about it she tried to give him the ten dollars she was supposed to donate to the school band travel fund, but Logan wouldn't take it. He said accepting money would make him a professional hit man, which might not look good when he tries out for pro baseball.

Willow Bend Road takes a big loop through some old farmland before it ends up back on the main road about a block from my school. I'm coming down the hill at the top of the loop when the bay horse sees me and trots to the fence to meet me. I know she's a bay because that's what *The Horse Encyclopedia* calls horses that are brown with black manes and tails. I sit on the top rail at the gateway and feed her carrot sticks from my lunch bag. Mom is happy that I want carrot sticks instead of Cheezies or Oreos; she says that if I eat carrot sticks I can reduce my risk of developing type one diabetes. She doesn't know I feed them to the horse. I don't care much about getting enough fiber. What I want is lots of protein to help me grow faster.

I have named the horse Nickers. She is very sweet. Today I have decided to ride her.

I hang my backpack on the post and unzip the main compartment. I have to dig around in the bottom to find my old skipping rope, hidden where no one can see it—I am teased enough without Amber finding it and thinking I still play skipping.

Nickers waits patiently beside me. I know I can't get the rope around her head like a real halter or bridle, and I don't have a bit anyway. So I loop it around the base of her neck and put a knot in it. Then I stand on the middle gate rail, lift my right leg over her back and push myself aboard.

Nickers just stands there. I'm a long way off the ground. I feel higher than when I was sitting on the top of the gate, even though I'm not.

I hang onto my skipping rope and wiggle my bum on her back.

Nickers stands there some more.

And that's enough for me.

I slide off, untie my skipping rope and give her another piece of carrot from my pocket. "Thanks, Nickers," I say. "That's a good start! We'll do some more later when I'm not so nervous."

I'm not sure about telling her I'm nervous. Mom says honesty is always the best policy, but Dad says never let an animal see your fear. Maybe Mom is talking about people and Dad is talking about dogs. Neither of them knows about horses. They don't know where I got my interest in horses. All I know is I was born this way.

I bike home the long way from school too (C+ in math. Not bad.). But when I see Nickers I don't feel brave enough to try riding her again, so I give her the last piece of carrot and go home.

After dinner I pretend to be doing my homework in my room but really I'm reading *The United States Pony Club Manual of Horsemanship* that I found at the thrift store. I need to learn how to ask Nickers to walk when I'm riding her. The manual says I'm supposed to squeeze with my calves and push with my seat. I put a couple of pillows between my legs to practice and that is when Mom comes in. She doesn't even knock.

"Oh dear," she says.

She backs out of my room, closes the door, opens it and comes in again.

"How was school?" she asks.

I put the pillows back on the bed. "I got a C+ on my math test."

She's looking at the Pony Club manual open on my desk. She slips a finger under the spine and lifts it, like she's looking for something underneath it. Something even worse.

She has that non-look on her face she uses when she's fulfilling some serious parental responsibility or when she's talking to one of her patients on the phone. What does she think I was doing?

She looks at the pillows.

"I was practicing riding," I tell her.

She sits on my bed. I know she's relieved even though she's trying not to show it. "Of course," she says.

I nod several times. Whatever she thinks I was doing, I don't want to hear about it.

She says, "And if it was something else, you would tell me and we would talk about it."

"Something else?" I say, which is a mistake—I see it as soon as she folds her hands in her lap and takes a deep breath. So quickly I add, "Of course, I know I can always talk to you, Mom."

"About anything," she says.

"Right," I say.

"I know that puberty is a challenging developmental stage," she says.

"Mom—I know." I try not to sound too exasperated with her, but I hate the puberty lecture and will do anything to avoid hearing it again. She has me so prepared with information about changing hormone levels and increased awareness of boys that I have completely lost interest. Not that I have ever had any interest. Boys have never been as interesting to me as horses.

Her eyes sweep slowly around my room. Maybe she is looking for a boy hidden somewhere?

"Well, I'll leave you alone then."

After she's gone, I lie on the floor and try to distract myself by doing my stretching exercises. I always feel upset after Mom raises the puberty issue because I'm reminded that I'm not there yet. I'm stuck in latency, the previous developmental stage. I am a teenager with the body of an eight-year-old. I don't mind so much that I'm not developed, but being short is a big problem for me. That's why I stretch, any chance I get. But what I really don't understand is why my parents don't say anything. It's as though my mom is pretending I'm a normal, struggling teenager while my dad pretends I'm still a child. No wonder I feel confused all the time.

CHAPTER TWO

I'm galloping. I can feel the wind on my face and I hear the pounding of hooves. It's fun, and it's so easy! Look, no reins, no saddle, and we're in the middle of a galloping herd of horses. There are blacks and greys and pintos, flying manes and tails. And look how stable I am! I'm not falling off, I'm not sliding, I'm in perfect relaxed wonderful blissful balance. I could go on like this for miles and miles and miles.

What was that clicking sound? It was exactly like the noise my clock makes before—

I open my eyes. The light is coming in around the curtains. I shut off the alarm and fall back into the pillows, and try to think of anything in the upcoming day that will be even half as interesting and exciting as my dream.

At the breakfast table Mom has left the Community Recreation Guide open on my placemat. She's used a yellow hi-liter to mark a gymnastics club. Gymnastics. Somehow running around indoors and wearing tights doesn't seem like real sports to me. Plus I know how I'll look in a leotard. There'll be no hiding it.

"It will be so good for your self-esteem. Why not try?"

says Mom. She's got that pleading look that makes me feel all heavy inside. If I say no, I'll disappoint her. If I say yes I'm stuck doing something that isn't me. "What do you think, Tony? Don't you think Sylvie would be great at gymnastics?"

"I sure do," says Dad, so fast that I know they've set the whole thing up. There's no hope, I'm sunk. Gymnastics it will be.

"Your dad can take you after school," says Mom. "It'll be nice for the two of you to have something to do together."

"Dad's going to take gymnastics with me?"

"No, Pumpkin. But he can drive you there and watch your class, then bring you home for dinner."

I look at Dad. He's got this strange little wobbly smile on his face but he nods encouragingly at me.

It's a done deal, though I don't think he likes it any more than I do.

On the way to school, Nickers is at the gate waiting for me when I pull up on my bike. She stands still when I wind my skipping rope around her neck, and then goes sideways to the rail as easy as pie. I get my leg across her back and boost myself off the gate. I grab her mane and sit for a minute. I can feel her breathing through my legs; her sides go in and out. She's warm and soft and she smells like heaven. I take a deep breath for courage, then squeeze my calves against her and push forward with my bum, like I practiced with the pillows.

Nothing happens. Well, at least she doesn't move her feet. Instead she bends her neck around so her nose is on my toe. I pat her neck and she straightens out. "Oh, Nickers, I just want you to walk," I tell her.

And she walks. This big moving animal underneath me

is walking! It's nothing like my pony-riding dreams—I am lurching and sliding and we're only walking, not trotting and absolutely not galloping. "Oh my gawd," I say, "how am I going to make you whoa?"

And she whoas.

And I have an idea.

"Walk," I say.

And she walks.

"Whoa," I say.

And she whoas.

"You understand English!" I say.

Nickers takes another sniff of my toe.

"Take me back to the gate," I say.

Nickers straightens her neck then backs up. I think about what I said.

"Whoa."

She stops.

"Back."

She backs up.

"Holy cow!" I say.

Her ears waggle, but then she stops.

This is amazing. A horse that understands the English language. Who would have thought? This is enough excitement for me for one day, so I slip off her side, undo the skipping rope and run back to the gate for the carrot sticks. And Nickers trots up right behind me! She loves me!

I'm five minutes late for school. Mr. Brumby asks for an explanation and I can't think of anything. I'm sure not going to say anything about Nickers. Mr. Brumby says I'm flushed and my eyes look funny and I'm thinking that being sick might be a good excuse when Amber says I always look funny because of my ears. The whole class falls silent. I wish I could make a joke or that someone would laugh because the silence is like an acknowledgement that what she's said is true. I want to crawl under my desk and die but I can't. I'm trying to think about Nickers and make everything not bother me when Logan Losino lets out the loudest, longest fart I have ever heard in my life. Fortunately his desk is two rows away from mine. Everyone groans and screams until Mr. Brumby slaps the wooden pointer across his desk. Mr. Brumby still wants to send me to the nurse's office but I tell him I'm fine. I'm just fine. I am amazingly fine. I rode a horse.

I can't see Nickers after school because I have to go straight home so Dad can take me to gymnastics. This turns out to be okay though, because I'm the first one in the house and when I check the mail I find the new catalogue from Greenhawk Equestrian Supplies that I ordered for free from their website. I hide it under some Archie comics that my cousin Taylor gave me. Mom hates these comics, she says they are junk food for the mind, so I know she won't touch them and the catalogue will be safe there. Then Dad comes home and tells me to change my clothes. He says I can wear a sweatsuit, I don't have to wear Spandex for my first class.

Dad takes two calls on his BlackBerry while we're on the way to the rec center, something he wouldn't be allowed to do if Mom was there. She thinks it's not safe to drive and talk on the phone at the same time and Dad says if she didn't multi-task on the phone all the time no housework would get done. But I agree with Mom on this—there's not much chance of being hit by a speeding truck while talking on the phone and dusting—so without saying anything I give Dad's cell phone an evil stare and he puts it away but then he wants to know how school was today. He wants to know if I've got a boyfriend. These are things I don't like to talk about and he's usually not interested, so I know it's the long arm of Mom at work.

Ms. Hackney, the gymnastics instructor, says I can stroll around watching everybody and notice if anything in particular appeals to me. I recognize a few kids from school, but there's no one from my class. Some people are tumbling on mats, some are walking on the balance beam. There's a set of uneven parallel bars at the back of the gym that no one is using so I wander over. I feel more comfortable with fewer people around.

I look up at the tallest of the two bars and stretch, but it's out of reach. It's perfect.

I jump, grab the bar and hold on. My fingers barely make it around the bar. I lift myself up for a few seconds and rest my chin on the bar, adjust my grip then I hang down again until my palms sweat so much I lose my grasp. That's when my dad comes over, sent by Ms. Hackney, who insists that everyone must have a spotter.

I look at the lower bar.

"Hey, Dad, help me up here."

"Do you really think? I mean, shouldn't you be learning by watching the other kids?"

"No, Dad, really. Help me here, lift me up, I want to hang from my knees."

He stuffs his BlackBerry in a pocket and lifts me up so I get my knees hooked over the bar, then he lowers my shoulders until I'm hanging upside down.

"Now what?" he says.

"Nothing. It's perfect." I can feel my face throbbing from all the blood running to my head. I let my hands hang down and my fingers brush the floor. I look at my dad, who is upside down now and standing on the ceiling.

Ms. Hackney slides in beside him. "Well, Sylvie, you've gravitated to a very challenging apparatus. Do you want to see what else you can do?"

"No, this is just fine," I say, because it is.

"Would you like to try a flip over the bar?" I see her look at Dad who shrugs his shoulders.

"No. This is all I want to do."

"Well maybe next time, no sense rushing things," says Ms. Hackney.

"This is all I'll ever want to do," I say, to be perfectly clear. I don't want any misunderstandings. I don't want anyone getting their hopes up that I'm going to turn into an Olympic gymnast. I want to hang and stretch. If they let me do this, I'll be fine.

"There's a lot more to gymnastics than hanging off a bar," says Ms.Hackney. She doesn't sound pleased.

"Not for me," I say.

Ms. Hackney turns to Dad and says, "She's a strong little thing—girls of her stature can do very well in gymnastics as long as they are sufficiently flexible. And I'd say Sylvie's as strong as some of the boys."

Strong as a boy? Well I don't mind that as long as I don't smell like one.

They turn their backs to me and have a little confab. Ms. Hackney will be saying something like she'll work on me and I'll come around. My dad will say no, she won't come around, because he knows me. He's known me a long time. He's known me since I was born, and along with my mom he knows everything about me. Well, almost everything. There's one thing they don't know, and even though it's only one thing it's a big thing, and I think about it every single day.

It happened when I was five. I can still remember it crystal clear even though I'm now fourteen. I was in the kitchen at Auntie Sally's house, the one she rented before the one that she's in now. I was so short, the countertops were level with my eyeballs. Grandpa was with me, he was visiting from Saskatchewan and I was talking to him about getting a horse because Auntie Sally had acreage.

"Half an acre isn't really acreage, Pipsqueak," he told me.

"They've already got it mostly fenced, we could close in that one bit below the compost pile and there'd be a paddock."

"Well you've got a good point there. Too bad the city bylaws won't allow livestock in this neighborhood."

"We'd have to tell them?"

"How long do you think you could hide a horse?"

The countertop was a sunny yellow colour with pale flecks and black seams at the edges. When I leaned against the lower cupboards the door handles dug into my back. I remember thinking that maybe I'd never have a pony. It was all I wanted, even then.

"I'll make you a deal," said Grandpa. "When you grow up to be as tall as my shoulder, if you're still interested in horses, I'll buy you one."

I checked his face and he was serious, he wasn't kidding around. Then I looked at his shoulder. It was a long way up there. A really, really long way. But still.

"Okay," I said.

I didn't tell Mom or Dad. Any time I hint around about having a horse one day, Dad says where would you keep it, then talks about how expensive horses are and how equestrian sports are elitist, which I thought sounded pretty good until I looked up elitist in the dictionary and saw it meant a "socially superior group" which reminded me of Amber and Topaz. And Mom always makes the same comment about me being in a "horse-crazy stage", as though it's another developmental stage and I'll grow out of it. But I know I won't. Not in a million years.

❄

After dinner I try a couple of math problems then work on my pulley diagram for science class, which gives me an idea. I figure I probably won't be going back to gymnastics, but it has inspired me to investigate new stretching techniques. So I tie my two skipping ropes together, put a loop around my ankles, feed the line around the base of my bureau, across the room and around one of the feet of my bed. Then I lie in the middle of the floor, stretch my hands over my head, grab the loose end of the rope and pull. At first I'm afraid the bureau might topple over and crush me, which would be devastating for my parents, but it moves half an inch, then sticks. I feel the pull on my ankles at one end and a pull on my shoulders at the other and I am trying to figure out how to get the stretch down my back when Mom knocks and immediately pops her head into the room.

"Oh, hi, Mom," I say, trying to sound natural.

For once Mom is stuck for words.

"I'm doing a science project," I say. "About pulleys."

"Okay," says Mom. She doesn't look convinced. "But don't wrap anything around your neck."

My neck! Of course, I should have thought of that, it would be a much better way of stretching my spine without dislocating my shoulders. My neck is pretty short to begin with. Maybe if I put a scarf around it for protection and then the skipping rope on top . . .

"Sylvia." She uses her special tone. "Nothing around your neck."

"Sure, Mom."

Later that night, after I've gone to bed, I have to get up to use the bathroom and I see that lights are still on in the kitchen. I figure I might as well get a glass of water while I'm up but then I stop in the hallway when I hear Mom's and Dad's voices. They are talking very quietly so I know it has something to do with me. I slide down against the wall and sit on the floor.

Mom says, "There's an article in *Psychoanalyst Review* about girls and horses."

"You're kidding," says Dad.

The kitchen door is ajar, and I can see through the louvers if I find the right sight line. I can see Dad's feet. He's still wearing his good shoes. They are my favourites with rich red-brown leather that shines even in the shadow under the kitchen table. There are little leather tassels on the top of each shoe. I would love to have shoes like this, but Dad says they are extremely expensive so I have to wait until I am a grownup with a job and money of my own. I told him that I'm old enough to have a part-time job but he snorted like he didn't believe me, then said there was no reason for me to be in such a hurry.

"Apparently riding offers ways of fulfilling and working through wishes and fears that are displaced from parents," says Mom.

"How do they figure that?" says Dad. His feet slide back under his chair then perch on their toes. Ballerina feet.

Mom is wearing her lambskin slippers which are a million years old, all saggy and thin-soled, but I know she loves them—she'll never throw them out or replace them. She slides them out in front of her and crosses her legs at the ankles.

"Well, Freud identified a number of developmental stages—"

"Oh, not this again."

Mom starts tapping her toes together. "All right then, I can skip all that, but to put it on a practical level, perhaps she's afraid we're going to divorce."

Divorce? Why would they divorce? Have I missed something? Fortunately my dad says, "Where would she get that idea?" The tassels on his shoes are vibrating.

"I run into this issue all the time at work—lots of kids worry that their parents are going to break up."

Sure, but not my parents.

Dad grunts. He doesn't seem to buy this either.

"And I know you have no interest in the theoretical background, but it's also possible that riding is an early adolescent phallic activity."

I make a mental note to look up "fallick" in my dictionary. It doesn't sound like a bad thing, but then I hear Dad say, "Oh give me a break."

"And that it's a substitute for conscious masturbation."

Masturbation I don't have to look up. That was the topic of one of the more embarrassing talks I've had with Mom, so it's burned into my memory forever.

"She's thirteen," says Dad.

"Fourteen," Mom corrects him, thank goodness. "She can't stay your little baby girl forever."

Dad's feet go flat on the floor. "Why would I . . . you're the one who—"

"And while we're talking about this I should also warn you that, according to the article, there's a correlation between women's interest in horses and idealized relationships with unavailable fathers. Which is why I thought you taking her to gymnastics would be a good idea."

"Gymnastics is not going to work," says Dad. "All she wants to do is hang from the bars and stretch."

"See?" says Mom. "She's obsessed with becoming taller and growing up. She wants to be an adult. It's so Jungian. She wants to marry you."

"Evelyn," says Dad, which is not a good sign. Usually he calls her Evie, or when he's kidding around he says it more like "E.V." which he says stands for "extra voluble". I keep meaning to look this up but haven't done it yet.

"It's classic Electra Complex," says Mom.

"Oh right," says Dad. "So she's going to murder you and marry me, is that how you see it? Hey—isn't this like one of those Shakespeare plays?"

Murder my mother? Marry my father? Is this all code for something else? Because straight out it makes no sense to me at all.

"Well *Hamlet* of course, though the genders are reversed, but it's the same idea," says Mom.

My dad's heels are bouncing. "Have you ever considered, Evelyn, that perhaps your relationship with Sylvie could use some work?"

Oh, no, Dad. Don't say that. She's trying too hard already.

"Work?" says Mom. She can't believe it either.

"Well, not exactly work," says Dad. "You're already too serious with her. You're always psychoanalyzing her—"

"I do no such thing."

"Ever since you went back to school and started this new job—"

"That is so unfair."

"Couldn't you just play with her?"

"Tony, she is much too old for that."

"Well then, female bonding maybe? That way she'd have second thoughts about bumping you off and marrying me."

There's a long silence, then I hear Mom sniff. "Now you're being ironic," she says.

"I am not."

"Just once I'd like you to take my career seriously."

Dad's heels bounce some more. "You need to lighten up, Evelyn. You need to leave work at work and stop applying all that psychological stuff to your family."

"Well you certainly bring your work home."

"Only to the extent that I use my financial skills to manage the family budget."

"As I use my psychoanalytic skills to manage the family relationships." Mom's slippers move out of my sight beneath her chair. There's a great long dark gap between her feet and Dad's feet.

"There's no comparison," says Dad.

"There certainly is," says Mom.

I hate it when they're like this. I feel sick inside, even though I know they always work it out. It's worse that they're arguing about me this time, and not the usual stuff like whether or not to trade in Mom's car on something newer, or what to say to Dad's brother next time he asks to borrow money.

"Listen," says Dad, "I was only suggesting that you and Sylvie do some things together. I tried the gymnastics thing, now it's your turn."

"Like what?"

"How should I know? Girl stuff. Go to a spa. Join a gym."

A spa? This is getting ridiculous. I could clear it up by telling them that all I want to do is grow as tall as Grandpa's shoulder. I could stand up right now, walk into the kitchen and explain everything. But what would be the point? They won't believe me. And if they did believe me they'd disagree with the whole plan, call Grandpa, tell him not to interfere and I'd never ever own a horse.

"Aren't you afraid that a spa will be too expensive?" says Mom.

"Are you being ironic now? Because if you are I think that's completely not called for."

"Oh Honey, of course not," says Mom. "It's a good idea. Leave it with me. I'll think of something." Her right foot has appeared out of the gloom and snaked its way over to Dad's shoes. She drops the slipper and slides her toes up under the cuff of his pant leg.

"Ready for bed?" says Dad.

"Mmm hmmm," says Mom.

I take off for my room and shut my door. They always make up. They would never divorce.

I can't find "fallick" in the dictionary.

CHAPTER THREE

We are galloping along a beach and into the waves. I've never ridden a horse in the water before. I wonder if they can swim, especially if they are wearing metal shoes, though I don't know if my horse has shoes on or not. I grab the mane and bend to one side but the horse's feet are moving too fast going in and out of the water and I think hey, I'm riding, and I'm not falling off, and it's bareback, oh boy! And I have the most amazing thought: since I'm riding, I must be dreaming. I try to keep the thought kind of quiet so it doesn't wake me up. I pay attention to the dream, to the white mane of the horse, to the sound of the water splashing. And then I think, well, if it's a dream I'm not going to hurt myself, I'm not going to fall off, so I should have some fun! And we go farther into the water until I'm sure it's really deep and the horse must be swimming but we're going along smooth as silk. Suddenly there's another horse and rider beside us and I think too bad this is a dream, too bad this can't be reality and that's when I wake up.

I must grow taller.

It's Saturday. There's no wake-up alarm, and even though

it's only eight o-clock Mom comes in and sits on the edge of my bed.

"Hey, Sugarplum," she says.

"Morning," I say. I'm still feeling sad about the dream just being a dream.

"I thought we should do something special together today," says Mom.

"Oh yeah?"

She reaches over and I think she's going to straighten my bangs out of my eyes but instead I feel her lift a strand of hair from the top of my head and let it slide through her fingertips. "Do you ever think about putting in hi-lights? They'd make you look very grown-up."

"Mom, I prefer it plain, and simple." She knows this, we've had this discussion before, but I try not to sound impatient with her. I know she's had a lot on her mind.

"Your dad would really like it," she says, which reminds me of their conversation I overheard last night. Now I see where this is going.

So I say, "Sure Mom, that sounds like fun." My day is ruined.

I'm not even due for a haircut. I was at Magic Cuts only two weeks ago—this is where Dad always takes me, it's in the mall and they only charge $6 which he says is a sensible price to pay for a trim. Mom wants to take me to Madeleine, who is her own hairdresser. She works in a salon on Fifth Street. But when Mom phones after breakfast she's told that Madeleine is booked up for the day and no one else is available and I think I have a reprieve, but then the phone rings five minutes later and apparently Madeleine has agreed to fit me in at 11:15 because of Mom being such a special customer, so my day is ruined all over again, and I start to worry that maybe my life is ruined too. What will the kids at school say if I show up next week with a new image?

I try but I can't think of an escape, unless I can draw the line at a cut. Maybe Mom would be satisfied with that, a new style, something with spikes that I could comb out on the way to school. I focus on staying calm and don't say much as we drive to town. Mom says I must be very excited because I'm so quiet.

I have a moment of hope when Mom can't find a parking space in the lot behind the salon and she won't parallel park her car on Fifth Street because she says the spaces are all too small. It's ten minutes past eleven and I think we might miss the appointment when Mom finds a spot around the corner on Duncan Street, in the angle parking section. We climb out of the car and Mom makes me run down Fifth Street and we're at the salon right on time.

I've never been inside the place before. Mom always goes on her lunch break, or after work, if her roots need touching up. I've walked past a hundred times without being able to see anything because the window glass is so darkly tinted.

Hanging on the door is a black sign with gold letters which say "Appointments Always Required." A bell on the top of the door tinkles as Mom pushes it open and I'm hit with a wave of warm air scented with chemicals that remind me of the embalming fluid I smelled at the science fair. I look back at Mom to make sure it's okay to go in because she's always concerned about air quality, but she doesn't seem to have noticed and she nudges me through the doorway. Right in front of us is the tallest reception desk I have ever seen in my life. It looks like the hull of a ship. From the top deck I hear a man's voice say, "Oh hello, Evelyn, how nice to see you," but I can't see anyone until an alien creature leans out over the edge and peers down at me. He has a tattooed forehead, pierced nostril, pierced lip, and ears which are more metal than flesh. His hair is raven black and stands up in a plume over his head. At least I think it's a man. The voice sounded like a man's, but I'm not sure now because he's wearing eye-shadow and lipstick. "You must be Sylvia," he says, and I add tongue-piercing to the list.

This is someone who needs a better hobby.

"Hi, Bernard," says Mom, solving the gender mystery but creating another one because I can't understand why she would talk to him as though he was normal. She's always warning me about people like this and how the last thing she would want would be for me to hang around with any of the Goth kids at school because they're into black magic and spiritualism.

Bernard sashays out from around the edge of the desk and pats me gently on the head. "Come along, we can take you right down, follow me. Are you staying, Evelyn? Will you be wanting a coffee? That's black with no sugar?"

We follow Bernard obediently past a row of chairs filled with caped customers. I smell hairspray on top of everything else. My nose is stuffing up.

"Sylvia—that means Goddess of Nature, does it not?" says Bernard, which is news to me. He doesn't wait for a response, but continues walking and chattering like an exotic jungle bird until we arrive at an empty chair near the back of the room. He takes another long look at me then slides an armful of towels off a shelf and arranges them like a cushion on the chair before he swivels it around for me to sit in. "These chairs aren't very comfortable if you're not as well padded as some of the older ones," he whispers in my ear. His eyes move to a large lady in the next chair and then back to me again. Bernard is nice.

Madeleine is nice too. I like her right away because she doesn't look like the other hairdressers—she looks more like she could use a good hairdresser, as though she doesn't care how she looks, as though she thinks other things are more important. She has snapshots of dogs and cats stuck all around the edges of her mirror. No horses, but she's obviously an animal person so I know I can relax. Maybe I can escape with a trim, maybe she'll see that I'm not the sort of person who needs to dye her hair and draw attention to herself.

She runs her fingers firmly across my scalp. "Lovely head of hair. Look at that shine. All you need is a better cut. You'd have more body and volume if we added some texture. Unless you prefer it simple like this? I could still leave it long enough so you could tie it back if you want to."

I see Mom in the mirror behind me looking like she's about to answer for me. But before she can say anything Madeleine slides her hand up the back of my neck. "Oh my. Look at this." She holds my hair to expose my neck. "Look how low your hairline goes here. Isn't this wonderful?" She drops my hair and fluffs it out. "It's like the mane of a lion."

"How about the mane of a horse?" I ask her.

"Oh, Honey," says Mom kind of sadly.

"Well sure," says Madeleine. "I like horses better than lions any day. So how did you manage to get a horse's mane? Your mom doesn't have one."

Mom pats her hair, then tucks it behind her ear. "Oh she was born that way. She always had a tremendous head of hair. We were thinking streaks or hi-lights today."

I sink into my cushion of towels and close my eyes and try to accept my fate. I feel Madeleine's hand on my shoulder and she says, "This is going to take a while, Evelyn. I think Marci is free—why don't you see about treating yourself to a manicure?"

After Mom leaves, Madeleine offers me all sorts of colour choices; she says I can put in streaks of pink or white or purple, but I say no thanks. I tell Madeleine I want to look as natural as possible, and she says she completely understands. So she puts in some faint auburn hi-lights on top and then because she's so nice and enthusiastic, I let her cut my hair. She promises to make it a bit more stylish without being outrageous. She's blowing it dry when Mom comes back and makes a big fuss about how great I look and wasn't this a fun thing for the two of us to do together.

Back at home I go straight to the bathroom to check myself in the mirror. I use a wet brush to take out some of the volume and end up looking more or less like myself. Thank goodness the streaks aren't obvious and I'm thinking maybe no one at school will notice, but then at dinner Dad says my hair is great and I look like a twenty-year-old and I try to show him I'm happy about this but really I am experiencing a hopeless feeling, like I'm trapped in the wrong life. I try to do what I usually do when this happens and think of something in the future that I can look forward to and I can only come up with two things (other than growing to Grandpa's shoulder)—one is seeing Nickers, and the other is having more riding dreams, and actually the riding dreams are even better than seeing Nickers because at least I can't hurt myself, there's no falling off, all there is is fun.

So after we've cleared up from dinner I tell Mom and Dad I want to go to bed early and boy is that a mistake.

They take my pulse and my temperature. I get the "puberty is a difficult stage" talk again and something about hormones and do I have any abdominal cramps. They review everything I ate during the day, looking for possible allergic reactions.

"Maybe it's the hair dye?" I suggest.

"Well I suppose . . . " says Dad.

"That would be a shame," says Mom. "You look so pretty with hi-lights."

"Oh well," I say.

"Look, I rented a movie for us to watch together tonight," says Dad.

It is too much to hope that it is *The Black Stallion* or *The Silver Stallion* or even *Pride and Prejudice*, all great horse movies, but even so I'm a little bit excited until Mom says, "We thought you might like to see the *Star Wars* series. We rented part one for tonight. There are some great archetypal characters I think you'll enjoy."

"Plus the special effects are great. Well, considering when it was made," says Dad.

I know there won't be any horses.

"I think I'll go to bed and read," I say. "But thanks."

I go to my room and climb into bed but I don't exactly read. I skim a few pages of the Greenhawk Equestrian Supplies catalogue but only because I'm hoping this will help me dream about horses. I tuck it back under the Archie comics and try to fall asleep. I try so hard that it backfires on me and I lie there with my eyes wide open watching the light from the streetlamp leak in around the edges of my curtains. My hair smells funny. Actually, it stinks.

Mom and Dad finish watching their movie and head off to bed.

And I lie there.

CHAPTER FOUR

I'm on a bay horse. The mane is black in my fingers and the coat is a glossy red-brown. We're only walking, nothing dramatic or exciting, except that just being on a horse is exciting. And it's dark out, so that makes it dangerous. But it's not dangerous, because I'm riding and therefore it must be a dream. On my right is another horse, and riding the horse is a woman I don't know. She has thick, wavy ash-blonde hair and she kind of glows so I can see her even though it's night time.

"Nice hi-lights," she says, which is a little alarming, but funny too.

I laugh.

"The smell goes away," she says, which is too much. I stop laughing.

"You're being very patient," she says. "And the stretching is a good idea, but we think it's time you did more. They're not catching on—your parents, I mean."

This is totally freaky. I'm not used to someone talking to me in my dreams about my real life.

She looks at me closely and says, "It's okay. There's nothing to be afraid of. Stay in the dream. Notice the horse."

"Okay," I say. I gaze down at my horse, the black mane, the pointy brown ears with black tips, there must be a moon for me to notice all this. There's so much light that I can see how similar this dream horse is to Nickers, she's the same colour, and I seem to be the same distance off the ground, and she feels the same under my bum, I can barely feel the ridge of her spine underneath me, and then she turns her head and sniffs my naked toes and I see it is Nickers. I am riding Nickers, in the night, in my bare feet and I am so excited that I wake up, but even when I'm awake I can hear the woman saying again, "Notice the horse." And my toes feel the warmth from Nickers's breath.

After breakfast, while Dad plays a round of golf, Mom drives me to her sister's house. She thinks it will be fun for me to have a visit with my cousins. My cousins don't like me. Well, that's a bit strong. It's more that we don't have anything in common so they hardly notice me. Plus they are all taller than me so even when they do notice me they treat me like a baby. Even Erika, and she is only ten. Taylor is fifteen and Stephanie is way older, she must be nineteen. Luckily, she is away at university so I'll only have the two younger ones to deal with. They do highland dancing and ballet, and they like wearing makeup. The only way they'd enjoy my visit is if I let them do a makeover on me. I hope that isn't in the plans.

Still, the drive over provides a good opportunity to quiz Mom.

"Mom, do you ever have dreams where you know you're dreaming?"

"No, but that sounds like fun, Pumpkin."

"It doesn't mean I'm crazy?"

"Oh no. It's called lucid dreaming. I've read about it but never been able to do it."

"You mean you tried?"

"Oh, a couple of times, when I was younger. Have you been able to do it?"

"I think so. Sort of."

"Good for you, Honey."

"And last night someone I didn't know was talking to me."

Mom smiles at me. "That would be your subconscious, Sweetie. One part of your brain talks to another part of your brain at night to sort things out."

"Even in a lucid dream?"

Mom nods. "Oh yes. Definitely."

I'm not so sure about this, but we've pulled into the driveway at Auntie Sally's and their dog Bunga is jumping on the car door and Mom is saying thank goodness we're not in your father's car, so that is the end of the discussion for now.

Auntie Sally tells me the girls are in Taylor's room and I can go play with them there.

"Play?" I say, but no one's listening—Auntie Sally wants to show Mom her new tattoo and is dragging her into the bathroom. Auntie Sally never seems to understand that just because I'm shorter than Erika and wearing her hand-me-downs, doesn't mean that I'm still a child. "I don't play," I tell their departing backs. "I hang."

I tap on Taylor's door but there's so much laughing and giggling and screaming going on inside no one hears me. I wouldn't have thought that two girls could make so much noise, but I also hope they haven't invited any friends over—I feel left out enough without any extra competition. I knock harder, then open the door and poke my head in. Erika takes one look down at the top of my head, yanks open the door and runs out yelling, "Mom, it's not fair, Sylvie got hi-lights why can't I?" So I guess it's not as subtle as I'd hoped.

Taylor's bedroom is a masterpiece of pink on pink on pink. Who would have known that pink came in so many shades? The only relief comes from the splashes of white from all the unicorns. Taylor is a unicorn freak. Even her bedspread has a huge white unicorn prancing across the middle of it. Her lamp is a unicorn. She has four unicorn posters on the wall and unicorns on her curtains.

"Wow," says Taylor. Since she's the middle child Mom says she'll be the best listener and the peace-maker, probably because Mom was the middle child in her own family. Auntie Sally is the baby. Uncle Brian was the oldest. Taylor picks up a strand of my hair in her fingertips. "How did you manage that?"

"It wasn't my idea. Mom wanted a female bonding thing and took me to her hairdresser."

"Oh poor you," says Stephanie from where she's lounging on the bed. University seems to have made her even more sarcastic than she used to be. "It must be tough there at the center of the universe in Only-Childsville."

"Well think about it, Stephanie," says Taylor. "How would you like having all of Mom's attention all the time? With no dilution?"

Stephanie shrugs. She is reading a fashion magazine which is open beside her and obscuring the horn of the unicorn on the bedspread. The unicorn ends up looking instead like a fairly reasonable horse, which as far as I'm concerned is a huge improvement.

"I thought you were away at university," I say.

Stephanie turns a glossy page. "Reading week."

"And you can read anything you want?"

She gives me her disgusted look. "Sylvie, you are so naïve."

Taylor says, "Stephanie, she's fourteen." She makes it

sound like it was an ice-age ago that she was fourteen herself, but I know it's been less than a year. I don't want to say anything though, because Taylor is the only one who stands up for me. She turns to me and says, "Don't worry about her, Sylvie. Stephanie's upset because her boyfriend broke up with her."

"Oh right, tell everyone," says Stephanie.

"He wasn't good enough for her anyway," says Taylor, which puts Stephanie on mute. "Show her the hickey he gave you, Steph."

Stephanie crosses her eyes.

"Plus she's embarrassed because Mom went to Stephanie's tattoo studio."

"She is such a wannabe," moans Stephanie.

"She wants to be one of us—she wants to be a teenager," explains Taylor.

"Unlike your mother, Sylvie," says Stephanie, "who is so desperate for you to become one of them. Hi-lights," she sniggers.

Taylor butts in before I can leap to my mother's defense. "So how is life anyways, Sylvie? What's new with you?"

My life disappears before my eyes. Other than the ridiculous hi-lights, there's nothing new. There's not even anything old to report that would be of interest to the socially sophisticated glamour sisters.

"I've started a new ballet class," says Taylor. She lifts an elegant slender leg and points a toe to the ceiling. "I've grown an inch in the last month."

That catches my attention big-time. "Ballet makes you grow faster?"

"Of course. It helps lengthen and strengthen the spine."

Stephanie stretches and yawns. "You're not the ballet type though, are you. You're more the peewee hockey kind of athlete."

"Stephanie, you are so mean," says Taylor. "Are you doing any sports, Sylvie?"

I shake my head. There is only one sport for me, and I'm not doing it. "I tried gymnastics." Taylor looks at me with such interest that I can't help myself. "I didn't like it though. I want to ride horses. That's all."

"Ha!" says Stephanie. "Like Uncle Tightwad is going to pay for that."

"Stephanie!" says Taylor.

Stephanie says, "I looked into it when I was younger. I wanted to ride then too. But it's so expensive—lessons, tack, vet bills. Cool clothes though—I love the tall black leather boots." She bounces her eyebrows meaningfully a couple of times; Taylor laughs and I pretend to, but really I don't get it.

"Grandpa will buy me a horse," I say. I have no idea why I'm telling them my special secret.

"Holy bananarama," says Taylor.

It's too late, but I say, "It's a secret. And not until I'm taller."

"That means not until you're post-puberty, have discovered boys, and don't want a horse any more," pronounces Stephanie.

Taylor glares at her. "Stephanie, just because you're disappointed with your life . . . ."

"I am not disappointed with my life. I'm being realistic. You know how cheap Mom says Uncle Tony is, and how Auntie Evelyn has to drive around in that old car. You think he's going to fund equestrian sports for his daughter? Unlikely."

"But she's an Only. It might be different for her than it is for us. And remember Grandpa paid for my ballet lessons. And your plastic surgery."

"Which is private and personal, Taylor. Just because he won't buy you breast implants is no excuse for blabbing."

"I don't want breast implants," says Taylor.

Stephanie turns her attention back to her magazine. "Well you should," she says.

I know all about Stephanie's surgery anyway so she didn't need to get mean about it. Mom told me. It wasn't as if the new nose could go unnoticed, but Mom made me promise not to say anything. I try to look like I don't know what they're talking about. Fortunately, it is a familiar expression for me.

Taylor sits at her desk, where she's started a drawing of a unicorn. It's not very good, she hasn't put in the fetlock joints. I would have thought someone who was fifteen would know better.

Stephanie finishes the magazine and fixes me in her sights. I feel like hiding under the bed. "If you want to get a horse you'll need to mount a campaign," she says.

I'm stunned that my problem has caught Stephanie's attention and that, after fourteen years I have suddenly become worthy of her interest.

"I can do that," I say. I try to focus on a spot in the center of her forehead. Now that I've been reminded about her nose job it's hard not to look at it, and I don't want to see her hickey either.

"What have you done so far?" says Stephanie.

"I'm doing stretching exercises all the time."

"Do your parents know?"

"Yeah, but they think I want to grow tall so I can murder Mom and marry Dad."

Taylor looks up briefly from her drawing. "That's disgusting. Not to mention incestuous."

But Stephanie nods. "Carl Jung—from my Psych 101 class. Complete baloney. What you need is a business expert—like me. We did a module on guerilla marketing and I got an A because my ideas were so creative."

"Gorilla marketing?" I say. I'm imagining dressing up in a gorilla suit and can't see how this would help.

Stephanie nods. She goes on to tell me I have to stop being so passive and waiting for things to happen. The stretching is good, but I have to advertise more. I have to promote myself in unexpected ways, she says. I have to hit them when and where they're least expecting it. Then she lies back on the bed and puts her arm across her eyes.

I had no idea that Stephanie was so smart. She makes me wish I had an older sister, though maybe not a sarcastic one, but someone I could talk to about personal things that I can't talk to Mom about because she's too old to understand what it's like to be young nowadays. I gaze at Stephanie with new-found affection, though now it seems she has decided to have a nap. I guess I'm not the sort of person who is interesting for very long, which is too bad because something else is bothering me and Stephanie would probably be the one who would know the answer. I decide to take a chance. "Stephanie?"

"What." She's awake, but doesn't take the arm off her eyes. Awake but bored to death, that's what she looks like.

Well, it's too late to go back now. I have to ask her, I have to finish what I started. "Stehanie, what does fallick mean?"

She laughs and props herself up on one elbow. "I think you should ask your mom about that. Or look it up in the dictionary."

"I overheard Mom say it, so I can't ask her or she'll know I was listening. And it wasn't in the dictionary."

Stephanie looks surprised. Then she says, "How were you spelling it, dopey? Not with an *f*?"

Taylor, who lost interest early in the marketing lecture, rescues me. She adds another strand of wispy mane to her drawing and says, "It starts with *ph*. Try that."

Stephanie sniggers then lies back on the bed and turns her back to me.

Later, when I'm home, I look it up.

My mother is out of her mind.

CHAPTER FIVE

I am lying on the horse's back, with my toes stretched down on either side of her tail, and my arms around her neck. The right side of my face is pressed into her neck and mane. She smells like nothing else on earth, all warm and fresh and sharp and musty all at the same time.

"How do you like the help we sent you?" asks the woman with the wavy blonde hair. She is standing beside me. She could catch me if I started to slide off, but I know that won't be necessary. I am solid as a rock on this horse . . . therefore . . . I must be . . . dreaming.

"Ahh," I say. "Another lucid dream. Amazing." I decide to take advantage of the situation and do something I would never do in real life. I straddle the horse, grab the mane, clamber onto my knees, then stand on her back, right behind her withers.

"That would be easier if you were standing on her rump," says the woman.

And immediately I'm on the horse's rump, one foot near the base of her tail, the other six inches away. "This is amazing."

"For a real thrill, she should be moving."

"Giddy-up then."

"Keep your knees soft and you'll be fine."

And I am fine. I am a famous circus performer. If only I'd studied gymnastics a little bit longer I could have done some really fancy stuff, like somersaults and leaping splits, but for now, this is enough. It's a blast. Then I think about what the woman asked me, about the help they sent. It takes me a minute to understand. "You mean my cousins?" I'm losing my balance, I can't raise my arms to break my fall and—pop! I'm out of the dream and into my bed, lying on my stomach, face mashed into my pillow.

It's Monday, and my first day of gorilla marketing. My alarm hasn't gone off yet, and Mom and Dad aren't awake. I have a few minutes of privacy to phone Grandpa in Saskatchewan. There's a time difference, so I know he'll be up already.

"Hey, Pipsqueak. How are you?"

"Fine, Grandpa, how are you?"

"Old and creaky. What's new with you?"

"I'm calling about what you promised me when I was five."

"Promised?"

I know that old people have memory problems but surely he hasn't forgotten something this important. I'm disappointed, but give him a reminder. "About how when I grow as tall as your shoulder you'll buy me a horse."

There's silence on the line, then a throat-clearing noise. "Are you that tall already?"

"Well I don't know. I need you to measure yourself at the shoulder."

"I can do that. Give me a minute here, I'll get out a tape measure."

I hear him put the phone down and a minute later there's the rattling of a metal tape measure. Then he's back. "I put a book on my shoulder and made a mark under it on the kitchen door. It's five foot two inches."

"Do you know what that is in metric, Grandpa?"

"Well, no, I don't, but you could figure that out."

"And were you barefoot?"

"You can take off half an inch for my slippers. Actually, take off a whole inch." He pauses so long I think the line has gone dead. "And then round it down to an even five feet. Or whatever that is in metric."

"Thanks, Grandpa."

"How old are you now, Pipsqueak?"

"I'm fourteen."

"Right, of course you are, I knew that. What do your parents think of this plan? What time is it out there?"

"It's early. They're not up yet. They don't know. I tried to tell them a few times but they weren't very open to the idea."

"I see."

I don't know what to say. I know I'm being sneaky phoning Grandpa like this, and sneakiness is not a good quality, but from Stephanie's description, gorillas have to be sneaky.

"I think you should leave this to me," says Grandpa. "Is today a school day?"

"It's Monday, Grandpa," I say, then I think it sounds kind of mean, so I add, "Well, at least it's Monday out here. Maybe it's another day in Saskatchewan, because of the time difference?"

Grandpa laughs, then he says, "You go off to school. I'll give your mother a call later this morning and see what we can sort out."

"Thanks, Grandpa."

"No problem," he says, then hangs up, just like that. No goodbye, no I love you Pipsqueak. But it doesn't matter. I know he does.

I go down into the basement to Dad's work bench and find his tape measure. Back in my room, I measure five feet against the edge of my door and mark it lightly with pencil. Then I remember Stephanie's advice about self-promotion, and I use a purple marker to trace over the pencil mark.

I put the Pony Club manual on top of my head and make it as level as possible, then back up to the door edge. I slide out from under the book and draw a line underneath it, lightly in pencil because I'm not sure how accurate it is. Then I examine the distance between the gray line of pencil and the stroke of purple.

There's a lot of space there.

I would measure it if this wasn't too discouraging. But I remember the help I'm receiving, from Stephanie and Taylor, from Grandpa and the lady with the wavy blonde hair. And Nickers of course. Thinking about Nickers always makes me feel better.

It's raining hard, so Mom doesn't want me riding my bike to school. Dad will drop me off on the way to his office.

They haven't noticed the purple mark on my door, which in a way is a relief because it means I'm not in trouble for drawing on the paint. But according to Stephanie I have to develop an obvious campaign as soon as possible. I leave my door half-open, hoping Mom will straighten it out and notice.

I decide to work on Dad on the way to school.

"I think I'm old enough for some additional responsibilities," I say.

Dad glances at me, then puts his signal on to change lanes. "Go on," he says.

"I'm thinking of getting a pet."

"A pet."

"So I can learn to be responsible and take care of something other than myself."

"Pets are very time consuming. And expensive. Even if they're free initially, there's still food and vet bills."

Stephanie had told me to expect resistance but not react to it.

"I was thinking of starting with something pretty simple."

Dad sighs. "Like what?"

"A barnacle."

"Barnacles are not pets. They're crustaceans."

"Dad, anything can be a pet. Mom had a pet rock."

"That was different, that was a fad from the seventies."

"Well I think it's a good place for me to start. You don't even need to drive me, I can ride my bike to the beach and pick one up. Or maybe a few, so they won't be lonely."

We have pulled into the drop-off zone at the school.

"I really wanted a kitten," I say, "but I know it would trigger your allergies."

I hop out of the car before he can say anything. He drives off and I turn to face the school grounds. And that's when I remember my new hair. I've been thinking so much about my horse campaign that I've completely forgotten the teasing I'm going to get about my hi-lights. And sure enough, within seconds there's Amber staring at me and laughing and she's about to say something when Logan Losino comes up behind her, grabs her backpack and runs off with it. She chases him, screaming she's going to kill him, so I am saved for a little while at least.

Dad is late picking me up after school and he feels so guilty that he says we can stop at the breakwater on the way home. He asks me if I really want a pet and I say yes. That's when his cell phone rings. Before he takes the call, he says, "All right but the minute it starts to smell it's going in the garbage." I scramble down the beach and pick a rock with five barnacles on it, fill my water bottle with ocean water and head back to the car.

"Look, it's like a little family," I tell Dad when he gets off his phone.

"I don't know what you're up to here, Shorty . . . "

"I think tonight I'll Google barnacles to make sure I'm doing everything right."

He drums his fingers on the steering wheel while he looks at me.

"Do you want to help me name them?"

He puts the car in gear. "No, I'll leave that completely up to you."

Mom has a late patient and doesn't arrive home until six. I show her how I've set up the barnacle family in a Pyrex dish, one of the old ones where the lid had broken so we didn't use it much. Dad says he'll re-heat dinner if Mom and I want to Google barnacle care. This turns out to be a huge mistake. There's quite a description on one site about how long a barnacle penis is and how much effort male barnacles put into searching for the right mate. This is exactly the sort of metaphor Mom needs to launch into another puberty lecture. I would have thought she'd be too tired for this after a full day of work, and that barnacles of all things would be a safe topic. But maybe sex is everywhere. And maybe Mom is always going to want to save me from the peril of an unplanned pregnancy, no matter how tired she is. I'm only rescued from an extended lecture by Dad calling out to say that dinner is ready.

CHAPTER SIX

We are galloping again, so right away I know I'm dreaming. I'm catching on to this stuff really fast. Now the trick is to stay in the dream as long as possible before waking up.

The blonde woman is galloping on a grey horse right beside me. She's laughing and her hair is flying like the manes on the horses. She sits up a bit straighter and her horse slows down, and I notice my horse is now walking too.

"Wasn't that grand?" she asks.

"These dreams are the best."

She looks at me, eyebrows raised. "Good for you, Sylvia. You're figuring this out."

I smile at her. She is the first person to call me Sylvia without being angry. For everyone else it's always nicknames or Sylvie; they only say Sylvia when they're trying to make some point, like about my not tying skipping ropes around my neck.

"You're making some progress with your parents as well. I know it's not easy."

"Sometimes I get mad at them," I say. I've never said anything like this before and expect her to tell me I shouldn't be critical, but she doesn't.

"They are good people, but things have happened to them."

"What things?"

"Oh, nothing terrible. Life stuff. And then they start believing things."

"Like about puberty?"

She laughs. "Puberty, financial planning, family dynamics . . ." She checks her watch. "Oh-oh," she says. "Time to go."

And my alarm buzzes.

Mom hasn't noticed the purple mark on my door yet, and she hasn't said anything about Grandpa calling so I guess he forgot. I don't mind, I can work around these set-backs.

The money issue keeps coming up from Dad. I'm going to have to do something about it. I have $200 in my savings account, and don't know anything about money. Dad says you can use money to make money, which sounds pretty weird to me. I guess I have a lot to learn. I figure a good place to start is the market report on the radio, and then if I have any questions I can ask Dad to explain.

We're sitting having breakfast. The news is over, and the weather report, and they're just starting with something about the Dow-Jones Industrial Average when Mom turns to me and clears her throat and I have to hold up my hand and say, "Wait a minute, Mom, the stock report is on," and I lean closer to the radio.

Mom blinks several times and looks at Dad who pats my head but of course doesn't say anything because he's listening too.

When the report is over (don't ask me what they said, I can't remember) Mom looks at Dad and says, "I told you, Mr. Hamlet."

But Dad laughs and says, "Come on, Munchkin, I'll give you a ride to school."

Which is great because it's still raining like crazy, and after school I'll need another jar of sea water for the barnacles.

Because of the weather a week goes by before I'm back on my bike and able to see Nickers on the way to school. Boy what a shock I get.

Nickers has two friends, a chestnut and a grey. And there are new fence posts lying on the ground beside all the rickety old fencing. And there are markers with plastic tags stuck in the high ground in the middle of the pasture.

Nickers remembers me though. She whinnies when she sees my bike and comes trotting to the gate. The other horses follow her, but she pins her ears at them and won't let them near me. She wants me all to herself, which makes me feel great. I feed her all my carrot sticks. I'm not going to ride her while those other horses are around, it's too dangerous and unpredictable. It's different from a dream, where nothing permanently bad can happen.

School is fine. Well, it's okay. Actually, it's kind of boring, and most of all I hate lunch because I don't know what to do with the other kids. I'd rather find a quiet place to read or stretch, but I know I'd look like a dork. And besides, in a way I want to figure it out, and I want to fit in, so maybe if I keep trying to hang out with all the teenage monster aliens, sooner or later I will know what to say or do. I wish it was like before Amber and Topaz moved here, when I didn't even have to do anything special and I was popular anyway.

Thank goodness I have my friend Nickers. I miss seeing her for a couple more days because the weather is bad and then I have a dentist appointment. When I finally resume my routine and stop for a visit on my way home from school there's a cement truck in her pasture and some men are pouring a foundation. I hang my bike helmet on the gatepost and watch for a while. The middle of a pasture seems like a pretty dumb place to build a house. The three horses are watching too, but pretending not to. They put their heads down for some grass, look up when they chew, then put their heads down again. I call Nickers but she either ignores me or can't hear me over the noise of the men and the cement truck.

There are deep ruts and puddles in the soil from where the cement truck went through the gate. The dirt smells fresh and sharp where the turf has been split. They should have waited until a dry spell. In summer the ground is as hard as rock.

I'm standing there, staring at the ruts and feeling sad because life is changing around me. I can't see how I can possibly ever ride Nickers again, partly because it will be too scary to ride her when other horses are running loose in the field, and also because if there's a house in the middle of her pasture people will be watching all the time. Plus I have to face the fact that Nickers isn't an abandoned lonely horse any more. She has horse friends now and if the new fencing is any indication, someone is looking after her. She won't need me any more. I've been silly thinking I could ride her and make her my own. Probably all my plans are silly, there's no point in campaigning, I can't count on Grandpa because he's losing his memory, my parents are set against me—nothing is going right and nothing will ever go right. My life is over, I'll never own a horse, all I'll ever have is barnacles.

And that's when a pickup truck pulls in beside me and everything changes right back again. It's like I had a life, then I didn't have a life, and all of a sudden I have a life again. Because there's a girl driving the truck and she opens the door and slides out and right away, even though it's totally impossible, even though I've never met her before, I recognize her wavy ash-blonde hair. I stare at her, waiting for her to say something because when she talks I'll know whether it's really her, the girl from my dreams, I know I'll recognize her voice, so I stand there with my mouth wide open.

"Hey," she says.

It's her. I don't know what to say. What could I possibly say? But she doesn't seem to notice that I've been struck dumb as a fencepost. She leans on the gate beside me and checks out the horses, then watches the guys at the cement truck for a while, then studies the horses some more and finally turns to me. My heart is pounding so hard and fast I'm sure she can hear it, because this is too weird, that someone I have dreamt about could appear before me in real life. And so I start to doubt myself because really this can't be happening but she's smiling at me with the same friendly look I know so well and then she says something that totally confirms that she's the same person I've been dreaming about. "Hey," she says like a private joke between the two of us, "nice hi-lights."

And it feels so normal that I relax a little and force myself to lean on the fence beside her, like I'm just hanging out with my best buddy. "Well, yeah," I say. "My mom made me. I'm not really into it."

"You into horses?"

I nod. It's too much to say out loud.

"Me too," she says. She looks like she's into horses, but not because of her clothes. She's wearing faded jeans and rubber boots and a man's jacket that's tattered at the cuffs. I know it's a man's jacket because the name "Ted" is embroidered on the chest and below that it says "Valley Fastball Champs 2005". So I can't say exactly why she's so obviously a horse person. There's just something. And basically she looks wonderful, even better than in my dreams, and I can hardly take my eyes off her except that staring is so rude.

And she doesn't seem to care anyway. She grabs her long hair in her right hand and with her left hand fishes an elastic band out of the pocket of her blue jeans and uses it to bind her hair behind her neck. I like her even more because it's not a sparkly little pink elastic with butterflies on the end, it's one of those thick blue ones that comes wrapped around bunches of broccoli. "Live around here?" she asks.

I know all the rules about talking to strangers, but I don't think they apply to girls who ride horses. We're part of the same tribe.

"Yes, I'm over on Willow Crescent. In the subdivision."

"I don't suppose you're sixteen?"

I know she's kidding. Something else we have in common. Bliss. "Not quite. I'm fourteen. I'll be fifteen at my next birthday."

"Oh." She looks surprised, but only for a second. I don't blame her. I know I don't look fourteen. But at least she doesn't make a big deal of it. "I'm looking to hire someone to pick paddocks," she says.

She's treating me like an adult. I want to hug her, but I know that right now it's more important to act business-like. "What exactly is *picking paddocks?*"

"You put horse poop in a wheel barrow and take it to the manure pile for composting. We have to do it for parasite control." She sees my confused look. "Horses get internal parasites—worms—and they infect the fields unless the manure is picked up."

"Oh," I say, thinking about it. "I could do that."

"You're not very big. You look like you could blow away in a strong wind."

"Yeah, but I'm strong. They said so at gymnastics."

"You do gymnastics?"

"Once."

"I can't pay much. I could pay you with riding lessons when I get the ring put in, after the barn is finished."

"That's a barn?" Of course it's a barn. I should have known that. "Where are you going to live?"

"In a trailer for now. I'll park it behind the barn."

I like her more and more. Anyone who would build their barn before they build their house is my kind of person.

"I think Nickers will like having a barn," I say.

"Nickers?"

"The bay mare," I say. I love saying it. The bay mare. Off-hand, exactly like a horse person, as if I say it all the time.

"Ah. I see." For a minute she looks like she's going to tell me something, she has that adult lecturing look, but then it passes. "My name's Kansas—like the state," she says smiling.

"Coulda been worse, I guess. They could have called you Mississippi."

"Or Rhode Island."

I feel a giggle building up in me and squash it down. Really, I'm so happy to have found someone who not only likes horses but also jokes around like me that I figure if I started giggling I might never be able to stop. I tell her my name is Sylvia.

She nods. "I guess you'd need to get permission from your parents—about the job," she says, but she doesn't sound sure.

"I can do that."

"You wouldn't have to start for a couple of weeks. I need to harrow the field first to break up the old poop, and then build the paddocks for the other horses."

"That's okay." This gives me time to work things out with Mom and Dad, but really it's great, it will fit in perfectly with my gorilla marketing plan. Then it sinks in. "Other horses? How many?"

"I dunno exactly. I'm going to have a boarding stable. I don't know how many will come."

A boarding stable. A place to keep my horse. If I didn't know better I'd think I was dreaming.

CHAPTER SEVEN

The river isn't very deep but there are a lot of big rocks visible under the surface so my horse has to pick its way carefully. So okay, I'm dreaming. We're about half-way across the river when I hear a shout, and it's the girl with the wavy ash-blonde hair coming up beside me on her gray horse. I try to bring her face into clear focus because I need to figure out if this is Kansas or not.

"Whatcha looking at? Do I have mud on my face?"

"Who are you?" I ask. "Do you have a name?"

"That's not a good idea, Sylvia. I know what you're driving at but you don't want to be building bridges from one place to another. That leaves paths for others to follow."

"Well can I just call you Kansas, for my convenience, because you look like her and remind me so much of her?"

Kansas drops her head and looks at me through her eyebrows. "Oh boy," she says. "This should take about three seconds."

She's riding bareback, and suddenly I see tucked in behind her, holding her around the waist, is someone who looks a lot like Taylor. She's wearing a pink ballet leotard and black knit leggings.

"Holy bananarama," she says.

It's Taylor all right.

"What are you doing here?" I'm not exactly happy about this, having to share not only my dream but also my dream friend. "You don't even like horses."

Taylor's eyes are the size of tennis balls though not the same shade of yellow-green. "I wouldn't say I didn't like them. More like I'm terrified of them."

"Kansas, what's she doing here?"

"I warned you about the naming thing—don't build bridges, don't make links. Not yet, not until you know what you're doing."

"But you've been calling me Sylvia."

"It's your dream—so there's no bridging."

"But why Taylor?"

"Oh Sylvia—you've done it again."

I have disappointed her and it is crushing for me. She sees my crestfallen look and softens. "No, no—it's okay, it's nothing bad, but it quickens things."

"There!" shouts Taylor. She's pointing to a beach on the far side of the river. "Do you see him? He's coming out of the woods!" She doesn't sound terrified any more. She sounds ecstatic, as though she's found her long-lost best friend—or more than that, as though she's seen some famous singing star, or Jesus. She sounds like I would sound if Ian Miller, Captain of the Canadian Equestrian team, were to leap out of the woods in his red show-jumping jacket, riding Big Ben, who is now dead.

At first I think it is a horse that Taylor is pointing to, a white Morgan maybe, or an Arab-cross, all sleek and shiny and muscley, with a wavy mane that's so glossy it could be made of threads of silver.

Then I see the long horn sticking straight out of its forehead.

"Oh give me a break!" I say. "A unicorn?"

"That's what it looks like, all right," says Kansas.

"But I don't believe in unicorns."

That's when the unicorn looks straight at me and laughs— not a whinny, not a nicker; he definitely opens his mouth and laughs at me.

"I believe in unicorns," says Taylor.

"But it's not your dream. It's my dream."

"Not any more," says Kansas. She is checking her watch. "Thank goodness . . . "

And I hear my alarm buzzing but I'm not ready to wake up. "Wait a minute—you have to tell me what's going on here."

But Taylor has disappeared, the unicorn has gone and Kansas is smiling at me and waving. "Goodbye! Have a nice day!"

I reach for my clock and switch off the alarm. I lie there for a while, thinking, wondering if I should phone Taylor, but it all seems too dumb. And then I remember that it's Saturday. I never set my alarm for Saturdays. What's going on? I'm almost ready to believe some weird explanation involving powers from my dream world turning on my alarm, when I come up with a more practical possibility which spurs me out of bed and into my clothes in record time.

Mom must have set the alarm after I went to sleep. I need to escape the house before she captures me for another mother-daughter bonding experience. I have a quick drink of juice (okay, I admit it, I drink straight out of the carton, drain it and put it back in the fridge empty. I know I'm not supposed to but I'm in a serious hurry. Besides, Dad does this all the time, so Mom will think it was him.) I leave a note on the table, grab an old pickle jar and ride my bike down to the beach for some replacement water for the barnacle family. Once I'm out of the house I slow down and take my time, so that when I return home Mom has headed off to an aerobics class, and Dad is reading the newspaper at the breakfast table.

"Hey kiddo, I saved you some porridge."

I lift the lid on the pan and there's a grey shiny lump piled in the middle. I stick my finger in it, and it's not very warm.

"Thanks, Dad. I think I'll make myself an egg. It's a better source of protein anyway."

Dad doesn't say anything. I see he's deep into the business section which reminds me of what Stephanie told me about self-promotion.

I use a louder voice than usual. "But I better take care of my pet barnacles before I feed myself."

Dad grunts.

I retrieve the barnacle family from my room and put the Pyrex container on the kitchen counter. I tip it up and pour most of their water into the sink, then add half of the water I got at the beach. The rest I can keep for Sunday, which will give me a day free from biking. I figure I can keep the water in the refrigerator, but the jar has dirt and mud on the outside, so I remember the juice carton, rinse it out, pour in the seawater and tuck it into the back of the top shelf.

I check out the barnacle family, and they are obviously enjoying their breakfast. Their tentacles are out and waving around, picking up bits of food. At least I hope they are tentacles. I hope I haven't got five boy barnacles here, all with long penises looking for someone to mate with. I wonder how to tell the difference between a barnacle tentacle and a barnacle penis, and since I definitely don't want to talk to Mom or Dad about this I decide to check back on Google.

I slip off to the family room. Of course I can't have a computer in my bedroom because Mom and Dad need to monitor my access to make sure I'm not in some chat room hook-ing up with a seventeen year old boy from out of town who will talk me into running away from home with him and living off the avails of prostitution on the streets in Vancouver.

The news from Google is not good. Apparently barnacles are hermaphrodites, meaning that one barnacle is a girl and a boy at the same time. So my barnacles all have penises, among other things. This is difficult to understand. Actually, it's difficult to believe, and if I wasn't reading it on Google I'd think it was a ridiculous made-up story.

Maybe a hamster would have been simpler.

Which makes me wonder if the same thing can happen with other animals, whether they can be both sexes at the same time. So I Google hermaphrodite. Obviously this is a mistake. I peek into the kitchen to make sure Dad isn't watching, and he isn't. There are some very strange photographs at the top of the screen that I really don't want to know anything about, so I scroll down quickly and then click on a reference to a hermaphrodite pony who made friends with a donkey because none of the horses liked him . . . or her. This happened in England, where Dad says all sorts of strange things happen due to the inbreeding of the European royal families. But this pony had both girl parts and boy parts, like my barnacles. They named him/her Tootsie, the same as a character in a movie with Dustin Hoffman. I have to remember to ask Mom and Dad to rent this one for me, though I won't be able to look too interested or they'll get suspicious.

The pony is pure white with a long silky mane. He reminds me of the stupid unicorn I had in my dream, and I figure this is a good opportunity so I Google unicorns. It's really really boring. Fierce but good, selfless but solitary, mysteriously beautiful, neutralizer of poison, tame-able only by a virgin woman, blah blah blah. Nothing about whether they can jump four-foot fences on a cross-country course, or do *piaffe* or *passage*, or pull plows or work cows, or do anything really practical.

Frankly, I find barnacles way more interesting than unicorns.

I wonder if I can get barnacle curtains and wallpaper.

"Whatcha up to, Sunshine?"

It's Dad. I exit the unicorn site before he can read over my shoulder. I don't want him to think I've gone all flakey. "Oh just doing some research."

"You almost done? I need to check some commodity prices."

I slide off the chair and let him take over. It's his chair anyway, a special one he bought at Staples with adjusting levers all over it that I'm not allowed to touch because they're set up perfectly to support his back. Mom says when he sits in it he looks like Captain Kirk at the helm of the Starship Enterprise which I think is a reference from the previous century.

"My barnacle family is thriving under my care," I advise him.

"Hmm hmm." He wiggles the computer mouse, trying to get the cursor over the bookmarks tab.

"And I will be starting a part-time job soon."

"Mmmmm." He opens his bookmarks. There's a whole line of them that he hasn't organized very well because he can't remember how to manage folders, even though I've shown him at least twelve times. He drags his pen down the screen looking for the site he wants and leaves a snaking ink mark that Mom will not be impressed by.

"Which will be helpful in paying for the upkeep of my horse."

"Oh yeah hmmm." He clicks on a site which opens to a whole pile of text and graphs that I know could keep him occupied until next week.

This is getting kind of annoying and I feel a reckless urge that I can't stop. "Dad, do you know what a hermaphrodite is?"

His finger freezes on the scroll button. He turns and peers at me over the top of his reading glasses. "It's the same as bisexual I think. But you'd be better off to ask your mother." He watches me for a few seconds more, looks back at the computer screen, then with what seems like an incredible effort slides his eyes back over to me. "Why do you want to know, Shorty?"

I shrug. "I dunno." I better not tell him about the barnacles. He might make me throw them away. So I tell him about the pony, though I make it clear that it's highly unusual for ponies to be hermaphrodites, in case that could become yet another reason why I can't have one.

"Oh. Well," he says, and he turns back to the computer screen. "Give me a minute here, Munchkin, I won't be long."

I leave the room.

I retrieve my barnacle family from the kitchen and take them back to my bedroom. I slide them under my desk lamp and watch the tentacles and try to see if one of them gets long and inserts itself in another barnacle. I try to imagine being a girl and a boy at the same time, and whether any of your sperm could get loose inside you and make you pregnant. And whether it was possible to decide what to be for your whole life so that you could marry, or whether you would have to marry another hermaphrodite so you wouldn't have to decide—you could just switch with each other; sometimes one person would take out the garbage and cut the lawn while the other person spent all morning on the telephone, and other times . . . I try to imagine my dad spending an hour on the phone laughing and talking about nothing like he says Mom does with Auntie Sally. I try to imagine Mom pulling the starter cord on the lawnmower until she's red in the face and wet with sweat and yelling at the stupid effing Black and Decker. I think about Dad being pregnant.

I look up bisexual in the dictionary, but it's not much help so I'll have to put off doing more research until I can get back on the computer.

I hear Mom's car coming up the street. The engine has a unique sound, so I always know before she gets home. I haven't had breakfast yet, which Mom won't be very happy about. She'll probably get mad at Dad. If I stay in my room until lunchtime though, she might not notice. I could come out then and act normally hungry.

I pick up the Pony Club manual and after checking that there's no reference to hermaphrodites or bisexuals in the index, I re-read the section on stable management. I hear the kitchen door open and close as Mom comes in. There's quiet down the hall for a minute, then I hear a lot of coughing and gagging and gasping for breath, and I bolt for the kitchen all ready to do the Heimlich maneuver.

Mom is spluttering over the sink. In her hand is the juice carton. She turns to me and there are tears streaming down her face. What have I done?

"Oh Mom. I'm so sorry."

"You? What did you put in here?"

"Just some ocean water, for my barnacles."

She swivels and retches into the sink. She rests on her elbows with her head tucked in under the faucet. "She's trying to kill me."

She says it softly but I hear her anyway. How could she even think such a thing? Then I remember them talking about that Hamlet stuff.

"Mom, no, it was a mistake! It was just salt water!"

"Oh lord," she says, and retches again. She puts so much

effort into it that it looks like her stomach is going to heave right up out of her mouth.

Dad comes in and puts his hand on her shoulder. "You okay, Hon?"

She shakes her head. "Someone is trying to poison me."

"It was a mistake," I tell him. "I put my extra barnacle water in the juice container in the fridge." Then it occurs to me. "She must have drunk straight out of the carton, like we're not supposed to."

"You weren't trying to kill her, then," says Dad.

I stare at him. They have both lost their minds. Why would I try to kill my own mother? I am going to have to read up on Hamlet now to figure out what they are so worried about. I can see I am going to spend the rest of my life on Google trying to understand the adult world. "You can't kill people with salt water!"

"That's true enough. Evelyn, did you hear that?"

I go over and join Dad in rubbing Mom's back.

Overall I'd have to say that my campaign isn't going very well.

That's when the phone rings. Since Mom can't talk very well and Dad is busy comforting her, I pick it up.

"Hello Pipsqueak."

"Oh hi, Grandpa."

"I just remembered I was supposed to phone and talk to your mom about my promise to you."

"I don't know that this is a good time, Grandpa."

Mom is suddenly at my shoulder. Her eyes are red and swollen and she wipes them on her sleeve. "I'll talk to him," she says and motions that I should hand her the phone. Behind her I see Dad heading back to the family room and the computer. He doesn't look very happy.

Mom's looking pretty fierce. And kind of angry with me. This really doesn't seem like a good time for Grandpa to be promoting my cause, but I can't think of anything to do to prevent it other than hanging up. "Mom wants to talk to you," I say, stalling as much as I dare. "She's having a difficult morning. She swallowed some sea water I left in the refrigerator."

Grandpa laughs. "Well that was a silly thing for her to do, wasn't it? Let me talk to her, Pipsqueak."

So I hand Mom the phone.

"Hi, Dad," she says. Her voice is still gravelly from throwing up, but then she stops talking. Her eyes start streaming again and she turns her back to me and stands there, leaning on the wall, listening to Grandpa.

I head back to my room and do some stretching exercises while I wait.

CHAPTER EIGHT

I wait and nothing happens.

I expect there'll be some sort of immediate family confer-
ence, but no.

I hear Mom hang up the phone, then see her out my
window dead-heading the roses. Then I think she goes for
a walk.

At noon I come out of my room and offer to bake some
muffins for lunch, which Dad says would be a great idea.
I'm starving and need to keep my growth on track so I eat
some raisins and walnuts while I'm preparing the batter.
Then Mom comes in and goes right to the family room.
Fortunately I have finished with the mixing machine so I
can hear at least some of what they're talking about. Mostly
they talk too quietly, but I do hear Dad say something about
Grandpa being an interfering old goat and then Mom uses
some words that she's not supposed to.

Over lunch Mom announces that she wants to take me
over to visit with Taylor in the afternoon. I know from her
tone that she's expecting some opposition from me, but I'm

curious to know whether Taylor remembers the dream she was in, so I tell Mom this is okay with me.

She looks surprised. "You don't have to feel guilty, Cupcake. I know you didn't intend for me to drink that . . . stuff. At least not consciously."

"Evelyn, let's not get into that again," says Dad.

"Stay out of this, Tony," Mom snaps.

Dad puts another warm muffin on his plate, splits it, slathers on way more butter than he's supposed to, then carries it to the refrigerator, grabs a beer and goes into the family room.

"We're not supposed to have food at the computer," I tell Mom.

She sighs. "I think we should let it go for today."

Mom makes a phone call, we put the dishes in the dishwasher, then climb in the car.

Auntie Sally has a glass of white wine ready for Mom on her kitchen table. I am, as usual, directed down the hall to Taylor's room, where I am relieved to find only Taylor and no other sisters. So it doesn't take long for me to swing the conversation around to dreams and unicorns and to figure out that Taylor has no recollection whatsoever of being in a dream with me and Kansas where we cross a river on horseback and hear a unicorn laugh.

I think I've been pretty discreet. If I can help it I'd rather Taylor not know what I'm driving at, but I guess my expressing any interest at all in unicorns is unusual enough to raise her suspicions.

"I thought you didn't believe in things like this," she says.

"Things like what?"

"Oh, spiritual things."

"Spiritual? You mean like the magic kingdom?" I don't

mean to be sarcastic, but it comes out this way, probably because I'm nervous.

Taylor gives me a look of total patience and sympathy that makes me want to punch her. Then she makes it worse by saying, "Well, maybe you're too young to understand."

"I can understand all sorts of things." I decide not to mention hermaphrodites as examples.

"You understand things in the material world, but the spiritual world is different."

"My dad says spirituality is a bunch of flakey nonsense for people who can't handle reality."

"Your dad . . . " says Taylor, then stops and smiles, as though she's reminded herself to be kind. "So how's Stephanie's marketing campaign working for you?"

I know she's intentionally changed the subject, but the way she says it is almost as irritating as what she was talking about before. "What do you mean, Stephanie's campaign? It's my campaign."

"Stephanie's good at talking people into things. I've had to learn how to resist her, which is hard because she's older and used to getting her way."

"She didn't talk me into anything. And it's going fine. I like gorilla marketing."

She gives me yet another annoying sympathetic look, then her face brightens. "I know—if you want to learn about spiritual things, you should let me read your palm. I'm learning how, I've got a book about it." She slides a slim volume out of her bookcase and flings it onto the bedspread where it lies across the top half of the unicorn's eye, giving it a sinister expression. Taylor drags me by my arm and sits me beside her on the bed, then pries open my fist and holds it on her thigh, palm up. And doesn't say anything.

"What?" I say. Even though I do not believe in palm reading her silence is alarming.

"You've only got one line," she says. "You're supposed to have two. See, like mine." She offers her palm for comparison. She's right. I'm missing a line.

"What does that mean?" I ask.

"I don't know." She opens her book and flips through the diagrams. "They all have two lines—one's your heart line and the other's your head line."

"I don't like this." I wrench my hand away from her. "Can we do something else?"

She closes her book reluctantly. Then she seems to get a new idea. "We can play Ouija."

"Wee-gee?" This sounds like it might be French or baby-talk, and either way I won't be interested. But anything to keep her away from my palm. Maybe I'm an alien and that's why I only have one line.

Taylor goes to her computer (her own computer, in her bedroom, out of parental surveillance, talk about lucky) and pulls up a site: *Ouija—The Original Talking Board*.

"Watch this," she says. At the top of the screen is a box for a question. She types: "Who does Taylor love?" then places the cursor over a triangular section in the middle which proceeds to move about the screen pointing to individual letters that eventually spell MANY. "Hah," she laughs. "That's because I'm so spiritual and full of love!"

"You're moving the cursor," I tell her.

"I am not. I'm following the pointer on the screen."

"Maybe subconsciously you're moving it."

"Well you try it then." She pops out of her chair and swivels it around in my direction.

This is obviously a scam, but I sit in the chair and type in my question. "How long until I can get a horse?" I put my hand on the mouse and then follow the pointer which goes to the number one at the bottom of the screen then slides back to its starting point and doesn't move.

"One month?" says Taylor. "Wow, that's pretty soon! Your campaign must be going great! Ask something else."

I don't know what else to ask. I've already asked the only question that matters to me. One month? How is that going to happen?

"Find out about boys. Ask who loves you."

This is a dumb question, and I don't care really, but I type it in anyway and the pointer slides around the screen. N . . . O . . . N . . . E. Noone?

"No one?" says Taylor. "That's mean. That can't be right. Do it another way. Ask who you love."

I'm not liking this game. No one loves me? My question hadn't mentioned anything specific about boys and the answer, even though it's a total scam, feels like a dagger in my heart. However I can't leave it on a bad note, so I type in, "Who does Sylvia love?" and the pointer goes K . . . A . . . N . . . S . . . A . . . and before it can finish I am so frightened that I slide the mouse up so the cursor is on the big red X in the top right corner and I exit the site.

"What did you do that for?"

I'm feeling sick to my stomach. "I don't like this spiritual stuff."

"It's nothing to be scared of. It's not black magic or anything like that, it says so right on the home page."

I want to leave, I want to go home and be with my barnacles, but I know Mom won't be ready and I'm not in her good books because of the salt water thing and because of whatever happened in her talk with Grandpa.

"Look," says Taylor, "all you need is some protection and you'll be fine." She rummages in the top drawer of her desk and pulls out some white fur on a key chain. "How about a rabbit's foot?"

"Are you kidding? The paw off a dead bunny?"

"Oh well, right, it's more a good luck charm anyway.

And you need something in the way of a spiritual protector. That's what I like about unicorns. They are strong and good. Any time I feel frightened I imagine my unicorn is protecting me and surrounding us with white light and love. Try it. Close your eyes and imagine."

I close my eyes and see the unicorn from my dreams, laughing. My eyes pop open.

"You're not trying hard enough. You are a virgin, aren't you? Because only virgins can tame unicorns."

This is so disgusting that I refuse to answer. I have no plans ever for not being a virgin.

"Okay, just checking, you never know these days. Close your eyes. Imagine you're surrounded by white light and a beautiful unicorn is guarding you with his golden horn."

I try again. I see the unicorn. He's looking kind of smug but he's not laughing any more. There's white light all over the place and Kansas is standing on the other side of the unicorn with a hand on his back and I start to cry.

CHAPTER NINE

What a disaster of a day. Mom is mad at me for trying to poison her, perhaps only subconsciously, but still. Dad is mad at Grandpa. Mom and Dad are mad at each other. I have cried in front of Taylor, who will now think I'm even more of a baby than she used to think, and she'll tell her sisters and pretty soon everyone in the world will know. I'm exhausted, but also so scared stiff by that wee-gee game that I don't want to go to sleep. What if I have a dream with evil spirits that do something to me or take me away or kill me or eat my soul? What if I wake up a zombie or don't wake up at all because I'm dead?

I decide to stay up reading all night. I don't know how many nights I can do this before dying from lack of sleep, but I don't care.

Unfortunately, Mom sees the light coming from underneath my door and tells me to put it out and go to sleep. Before I turn off the light I move the barnacle family from my desk to my bedside table. I figure I can talk to them all night long and stay awake that way. There's a bit of light coming in around my curtains from the streetlight so I can see the dark outline of the rock in the white dish and the faint jagged lines of the barnacles under the water.

After I hear Mom and Dad go to bed, I sit up and throw off the covers because if I'm cold and not too cozy I won't fall asleep. But, as usual, the furnace has been turned down, so by eleven o-clock I'm feeling pretty chilled. I put on a sweater and a pair of socks. It wouldn't be so bad if I had a computer in my room like Taylor. I could stay awake all night playing Tetris and doing internet searches. Then again, why couldn't I do this anyway?

I crack open my door and sneak a look down the hallway. No lights, no noise. I tiptoe down to the family room where the computer is in sleep mode like everyone else except me. I turn it on and while I'm waiting for the start-up functions to finish I swivel in the chair and think through the things I need to look up. There's that Hamlet stuff. Unicorns I've had enough of for now, I don't want anything scary. Definitely no more wee-gee. That takes me back to barnacles, and I remember that when I'd looked up *bisexual* in the dictionary it hadn't been much help. So I type it into Google which takes me to Wikipedia and thank goodness this time no photographs pop up. But it's not all that interesting either. I find a reference to bisexuality in non-human animals and click on that, but there's no mention of barnacles. I go back to the main Google page for other sites, and there are bisexual playgrounds and bisexual chat groups and bisexual support groups. I blearily click on each one, then hit the back button because there's nothing that interesting. No bisexual ponies. As a matter of fact it all looks pretty boring. I am very tired. I can hardly keep my eyes open. Still it's a good time to do research with no one peering over my shoulder for a change, so I feel some need to take advantage of the time. After all, I have my campaign to consider, which leads me to thinking I could use some new ideas about gorilla marketing so

I type that into the query box and Google says, "Did you mean guerilla?" This is so embarrassing. All that time I've been saying "gorilla" and it's supposed to be "guerilla". Quietly I say each word aloud, wondering if people noticed me using the wrong term. They don't sound much different. I may have gotten away with it. I try to remember how many people I spoke to saying "gorilla" but I'm so tired my brain folds in on itself. I try to play Tetris but my coordination is off, and then I play Solitaire but this is even more boring than Wikipedia so finally I give up, turn off the computer and sneak back to my room.

As soon as I'm there I feel scared again, which wakes me up a little. Plus it's cold, even with my sweater and socks on.

I promise myself that I will stay awake if I only put my legs under the covers. I won't lie down, I'll prop myself on my pillows and sit up all night. There's a bit of light coming from my clock radio, not enough to read by but enough to look at the pictures in my equestrian supply catalogue. I retrieve it from the stack of Archie comics, then sit in bed and turn the pages as quietly as I can.

I guess I nod off for a second without knowing it, because I wake with a start and the catalogue is gone and I'm lying flat out under the covers and I feel with my foot that there is someone sitting on the end of my bed. A shadowy figure is outlined against the curtains. My heart is going a hundred miles an hour and I try to scream but I can't. I can't move a muscle, somehow I've become a paraplegic and I'm frozen in bed, exactly where an axe-murderer would want me.

"Hey." It's a woman's voice, which is not what I would expect for an axe-murderer. In fact it's a voice I recognize. It's Kansas.

I move my eyes around searching for an open window or door, but everything is sealed tight. I don't know how she broke in here, but then again I'm so glad to see her I don't care.

"Having a tough night?"

I manage a nod. The paralysis seems to be receding.

She smiles understandingly. I can see her face now, there is more light in the room. Maybe the moon has come up.

"There's something you should know about your barnacles."

She's using the same tone as Mom employs when she has a new sexuality metaphor to foist on me, so I prepare myself for the worst but it's as though she can read my thoughts because she says, "Oh no, not that stuff. I couldn't care less what sex they are."

I am so relieved I could hug her. It is wonderful to find someone else in the world who isn't obsessed with sex or boys.

She rubs my foot through the covers. "Barnacles are really just little shrimps."

I know that anyone else telling me this story would take the opportunity to point out that barnacles are just little shrimps like me, but Kansas doesn't do that. "Well, they're shrimp-like anyway. They're not exactly shrimps. But they are crustaceans, like shrimps are. One difference is that shrimps have armor that they carry with them. Barnacles do something else—they build a limestone house around themselves for protection and safety. Then they reach out into the water and kick what food they need into their house."

I remember reading something like that on Google.

"I'm thinking you've forgotten about your limestone fortification," she says.

"What fortification?" Hey, I can talk! This is great.

"Well you live in this good house, for one thing. And you have your own room with your own stuff in it. And two parents and an extended family who are all looking out for you in their way. And you've got me."

"Yeah."

"So there's nothing to be afraid of."

"Really?"

"Really. You are fine. Everything's fine. It's all on track."

"I get scared sometimes."

"Well that's sensible. And it's why we need limestone fortifications."

She sits for a minute so I can think about what she's said, and she rubs my foot, then she holds it tight and waggles it. "Now, the other thing you need to focus on is kicking more of what you need into your house."

"I'm doing the guerilla marketing." I pronounce it carefully to be sure she understands that I know we're not talking about big monkeys.

"There are more difficulties ahead of you. You need to come back and see me. In the daytime."

"But your stable isn't finished. And you don't want to hire me until you've harrowed your fields to kill the parasites."

"Tomorrow," she says. "Now close your eyes and go back to sleep."

And I do.

In the morning of course I have to bike to the beach for more sea water for the barnacles because Mom drank my back-up supply. I guess this will have to be a daily exercise since I can't store the water in the refrigerator, which will be inconvenient but will also show them how responsible I am. And besides, it's only five minutes each way.

I leave a note for them on the counter to make sure they get the point: *I have gone to the beach for water for my pet barnacles. I will be careful of the traffic. I will be home for breakfast. Love, Sylvia.* I put in the bit about the traffic so they understand that I am taking some risks which I would not have to take if they let Grandpa buy me a horse because I wouldn't have to ride my bike on the busy road by the breakwater.

When I return home they're still in bed. I leave the note on the counter anyway, and change the water for the barnacles. I watch their tentacles come out and kick food into their houses, and that's when I recall the visit from Kansas.

Wow. That was really something. She was in my room. I felt her holding my foot. I flex my foot inside my shoe and remember the sensation.

I realize I'm not scared of evil spirits any more, though I'm not exactly in a hurry to go back and play wee-gee with Taylor. Today I have to find my way to Kansas's place.

I eat two pieces of toast with thick layers of protein-rich peanut butter. Mom and Dad are still not up. I decide to make them breakfast in bed.

"What's this, Pumpkin?" says Mom when I bring in the tray.

"French toast. Your favourite."

Dad moans into his pillow, then rubs his eyes and says, "Good morning, Shorty."

"You shouldn't call her that," says Mom.

"I have to call her something from one of the food groups, is that it?" says Dad.

Perhaps this wasn't the best idea.

"I don't know what you're talking about," says Mom.

"All your nicknames for her are edible," says Dad, which is perfectly true but I don't mind.

"They are not," says Mom.

"How about I make you both some tea?" I say.

"That would be lovely, Honey," says Mom.

"See?" says Dad.

"Or coffee. I'm not sure how you make it, but I can try," I say.

Dad carves off a forkful of toast and swabs it in the maple syrup. "This looks delicious."

"It sure is," says Mom, nibbling on a bit of crust she's pulled off with her fingertips.

"I'm wondering if I can go off on my bike for a while."

"Need to get some more purgative?" says Dad, then coughs.

Mom has picked up her fork but stops with it poised halfway to her plate. She looks for a minute like she might stab Dad with it instead. She turns to me and says, "He's making a little joke about your salt water."

"She was probably hoping that wouldn't come up again," says Dad.

And Mom laughs. So I see everything's all right.

"I'm going to meet a friend," I say.

"Someone from school?" says Mom.

I think about that. Kansas is someone from on the way to school, which is not exactly the same as someone from school, but it's pretty close. I tell her yes.

"Well that's fine with me," says Dad. "Cause I think I'm going to have to lie down for a while after this breakfast. How about you, Evie?"

And they let me go, as long as I promise to be back for lunch.

CHAPTER TEN

The pasture where Nickers lives has been transformed. There's an entire new barn on the knoll in the middle. There's a real gravel driveway where the ruts in the grass used to be. Power lines run from a pole at the road to another one halfway down the driveway and then attach to the front of the barn. An orange extension cord snakes around the side of the barn and plugs into a travel trailer that I can barely see from the road. The three lines of saggy barbed-wire fencing that used to go around the perimeter have been replaced with five lines of taut white cord on upright posts; hanging off the top line is a bright yellow notice warning that the fence is electric. Posts are also in for a fence line that will create a large paddock off to the side of the barn, but the fencing hasn't been hung yet.

But the problem is that the old wooden gate rails have been replaced with a new metal pipe gate, and hanging on it is a plastic sign which says *Livestock at Large* and under that a smaller handwritten sign on cardboard which says *Keep Gate Closed or Die.*

I stand staring at the sign. What am I supposed to do? How do I enter without opening the gate? I could crawl through the pipes but there's no way I can shove my bike through and I don't want to leave it out by the road where someone could steal it. And I'm not going anywhere near that electric fencing.

That's when I hear Kansas yelling from the barn. "Come on in, Sylvia! Just be sure to close the gate behind you!"

Kansas is busy brushing Nickers, who is tied to a ring in the alleyway, when I roll up on my bike. The other two horses are out grazing. I lean my bike against the barn.

"Hey," says Kansas. "I wondered when you'd get here."

So she's been expecting me. Maybe she remembers being in my dreams even though Taylor doesn't. I don't want to ask her about it though, because she had warned me not to build bridges. If mentioning a name from the real world during a dream is a bridge, then talking about dreams in the day time would be more like a multi-lane overpass. I should probably let her bring it up. She seems to know everything.

"This horse hasn't been brushed in months. Look at the crud in this coat!" She uses a plastic brush to scratch at the mud caked on Nickers's legs.

"Doesn't that hurt?"

"Naw. He likes the attention."

"He?" I was sure Nickers was a mare, though maybe that was only in the dream version. I didn't think dreams worked that way, mixing things up so badly, especially when Mom said the purpose of dreams was to sort things out.

Kansas stops brushing and indicates up under Nickers's tummy in front of his hind legs. "See? He's got a sheath. That's usually a dead giveaway that it's a gelding. Unless there are testicles attached, which there are not in this case. Thank goodness."

I have a good look under Nickers's belly at his sheath.

Kansas stands behind the horse and lifts his tail. "Here's

another way you can tell. Have a look here then we'll go look at one of the mares."

We stand together and inspect Nickers's backside. Kansas slides her hand down between his legs and makes a fist. "Testicles would be down here somewhere." She looks at me. "How old are you again? Is this okay, to be talking about stuff like this?"

"My mom's a psychoanalyst. She's made sure that I know all the theory already."

"Fine then. Let's go look at a mare. It's important that you can tell the difference between mares and geldings and stallions because they have to be treated differently and they react differently too."

We leave Nickers at the barn and walk into the field to find another example. "This is Electra." Kansas points up under the belly. "See, no sheath, just little nipples tucked way back there."

I crouch down and have a good look up under Electra who continues to eat grass as though it is no problem at all that we are examining her private parts. It's a bit weird about her name; I remember Mom talking about an Electra complex. Maybe it's a common thing. Maybe it's a coincidence and there are lots of horses named Electra.

Kansas holds up her tail and I have a good look there too.

"What about the other horse?" I'm kind of afraid to ask. What if it's a mare and her name is Evelyn? Or a gelding named Freud? Or worst of all, a hermaphrodite named Tootsie?

"Photon," she says. "Same as this one. A mare."

"You don't have any hermaphrodites here then?" I don't know why I ask this, whether it's from relief or I want to show off.

"You're way past me on this one, Sylvia. What the hell is a hermaphrodite?"

"It's an animal that has both male and female reproductive organs." It feels good to be an expert, or at least to know more about something than the nearest adult, but I don't want to make the same mistakes that the adults usually make by over-explaining things, so I'm not sure how much detail I should go into. "There's a hermaphrodite pony in England."

"No kidding."

"And my pet barnacles are hermaphrodites."

"You have pet barnacles?"

"Yes. They're part of my guerilla marketing campaign to get my own horse."

"What's gorilla marketing?"

I correct her pronunciation, but gently, because it occurs to me that Kansas is the first person I've met who is older than me and doesn't have to be a know-it-all all the time. Then I explain. "Like soldiers sniping from the jungle and taking people by surprise with new information."

"Hmmm."

We have left the mares and are on our way back to the barn and Nickers. The sun has come out and feels warm on my back. I can hear frogs croaking from the ditch by the road and the smell of fresh horse manure wafts up from the grass. It's a perfect day.

"So you're pretty serious about owning your own horse some day?"

"Oh yeah."

"How long have you been working on it?"

I sigh, probably a bit dramatically, but it's also how I'm feeling—totally relieved to be talking about this with someone who understands. "I feel like I've been campaigning my whole life."

"Well I know what that's like," says Kansas. "I figure I was born wanting to be around horses."

"Me too."

"It's a disease," says Kansas.

I summon a serious expression like Dad does when he's joking around. "An incurable disease."

"Fortunately," adds Kansas.

Perfection upon perfection.

"We'll have to see what we can do to get you to your goal," says Kansas. "Though I don't know anything about guerilla marketing. What's the situation with the parents?"

"They weren't born this way. I must have inherited a recessive gene. My grandpa used to have horses in Saskatchewan."

"Is he on side then?"

"He says he'll buy me a horse when I grow as tall as his shoulder."

She stops and assesses me. "Any chance he's a midget?"

Anyone else saying this and my feelings might be hurt, but I know she's not teasing or being mean. She's being realistic. "Nope. I do stretching exercises all the time and try to eat lots of protein."

"Good thinking."

"My dad says Grandpa is an interfering old goat."

"Bad sign. What about your mom?"

"She thinks it's a stage."

"Still? A life-long stage?"

"Something to do with my sexual development."

"Oh lord. Not that old sausage."

Back at the barn she hands me a comb and directs me to the knots in Nickers' tail. She brushes, I comb, Nickers stands there with his head down, his eyes half-closed, and rests one hind leg.

"You know, Sylvia, owning a horse is a big deal. They are expensive to keep and they are a lot of responsibility. So for a lot of people, just being around them is enough. They don't have to own a horse. They take lessons, they ride horses that belong to other people, they take them to horse shows, even win fancy ribbons . . . ."

I shake my head. This is not the picture I had in my mind.

"Well, it's not my idea of fun either," says Kansas. "It sounds too much like dating other people's husbands."

This isn't how I would have put it, and reminds me uncomfortably of Mom's theory about me wanting to marry Dad. I don't say anything.

Kansas carries on as though she's in another world. "For some of us, horse ownership is about having a relationship with these animals." With her fingertips she strokes the horse gently around his eye. "Right, Hambone?"

"Hambone? You named your horse Hambone?" I was sort of prepared that his name wouldn't really be Nickers, but Hambone is much worse than anything I might have imagined.

"No, I didn't name him. He came with this name. Actually he came with the property. The mares are mine, but I inherited Hambone."

"Can't you re-name him? Is it bad luck, like re-naming a boat?"

"I don't know about bad luck. But he knows his name. How'd you like it if I re-named you?"

I think about all the names people have for me. What difference could one more make? I shrug.

"You don't like your name?"

"It's not cool, like Kansas."

"I thought Sylvia was the name of an ancient nature goddess."

This is what Bernard had said at Mom's hair salon, but at the time I thought he was crazy. It's different when Kansas says it. "Really?"

"Sure. I read about it once." She returns to brushing, creating clouds of dust as she breaks up the dirt. "Though Hambone is his barn name. His real name is from Shakespeare."

My stomach turns. Somehow I know what's coming next.

"His registered name is Prince Hamlet."

CHAPTER ELEVEN

When I get home I lock my bike in the carport and notice Dad in the back yard working in his greenhouse. This is something he tends to do when he and Mom have had what Mom calls a difference of opinion, so I'm not sure about going in the house right away. Mom will be in there being quiet, "thinking things through", as she puts it. I decide to take my chances on Dad. He might be grumpy or he might need me to cheer him up.

I push open the plastic-covered door. The air is thick with moisture and earth smells. Dad is peering at a geranium.

"Hey," I say.

"Oh. Hi, Sylv." There's a strained smile on his face.

"Are you in trouble?" I say it playfully because it's a family joke—him going to the greenhouse instead of the doghouse when Mom's upset with him.

He doesn't rise to the joke. "Well I was for a while, but that was straightened out." He still isn't smiling properly. "I think you better go in and talk to your mom."

His tone is downright ominous. I check my watch. "I'm not late am I? I said I'd be back for lunch and it's not even one o'clock yet." My heart is thumping like crazy and my palms are sweating.

"No, it's not that. Go see your mom."

Oh this is big trouble. What have I done? I didn't leave out any more sea water for people to drink. I didn't let the barnacles die and smell up the house. I didn't put any poison in the French toast. "Aren't you coming in?" I'm hoping for back-up, though I don't know why exactly, because the situation could as easily go the other way and I'd end up with two against one, the one being me. They have a parenting rule about "no piling on" but it doesn't always turn out that way.

"I'll be in later."

He isn't looking mad. More sad. Embarrassed. Something.

I catch sight of my bike on the way back to the house. I wonder about unchaining it and flying back to Kansas, but this is a fleeting fantasy. Sooner or later I will have to face the music, whatever it is. Maybe it isn't about me. Maybe one of my parents has a fatal disease. Or they are getting a divorce.

There is a tuna fish sandwich waiting for me on the table when I arrive in the kitchen. There are pickles in it, and I can see extra mayonnaise dribbling out the side. She's made it exactly the way I like it best. What is going on?

Mom is trying to look happy but I can see the effort it is taking by the way her lips quiver in the corners. This is very confusing. Am I in trouble or not?

"Hey. What's up?" I try to sound innocent, which I am, though I don't feel like it.

"Nothing, Sylvie." Not Honey, not Sweetie, not Cookie or Cupcake. This is very bad. "Eat your sandwich. Then I thought we could have a talk."

I don't know how I can eat a sandwich when my stomach

is literally tied in a knot, but I sit down and nibble on a crust. A chunk of celery falls out from between the pieces of bread and lands in a puddle of tuna juice on the plate. I figure I can eat the celery, it won't be dry like the bread, it won't stick in my throat and choke me to death, so I pick it up and shove it in my mouth and chew.

Mom has turned her back. She is wiping down the already immaculate counter tops. Then she grabs a box of baking soda from the cupboard, half-empties it in the sink and starts to scrub.

I swear it takes me twenty minutes, but I finish the sandwich and half the glass of milk and then Mom says we should go in the family room.

She takes me to the computer. She opens the web browser. And clicks on the history tab. And scrolls down.

There are all the sites I visited last night. The ones I was mostly too tired to read but clicked on them anyway.

"Do you want to talk to me about this?" says Mom.

I am so frozen by the apparent seriousness of the matter that I can't think straight, and have no idea whatsoever what I should be saying.

"You can't deny it, Sylvie. I've already talked to your father so I know that it wasn't him visiting these sites."

Well of course not, he has no interest in guerilla marketing or barnacles or ponies.

"Not that you have to talk to me. If you want to talk to someone else, that will be fine, I can find a professional, one of my colleagues perhaps, or if you prefer I will find someone for you to talk to that I don't know."

Some kind of crustacean expert I am thinking. But then I think about how sneaky that whole guerilla marketing stuff is and that maybe it's worse than sneaky maybe it's downright dishonest and I shouldn't have been doing it and now she's found out, it was the last stuff I looked at on the net and now she's disappointed in me.

I hang my head. "Stephanie told me about it. She's studying it at university."

"Are you telling me you have no personal interest in these topics?"

"Well no, not exactly." I'm not sure this is the right time to come clean on the details of my marketing campaign.

"You can trust me, Sylvie. I'm aware that puberty can be an extremely confusing stage, and I also know that sexual preference is determined very early. Your Uncle Brian—." She stops abruptly and I take a peak up at her. Her face has gone all red. She sniffs, takes a deep breath, lets it out, and starts again. "I don't mind that you are searching for answers, but the internet may not be the best source of information. Nor for that matter is someone taking a first-year psychology course."

Okay, I must be really slow. So this has nothing to do with marketing campaigns. It's one of these puberty things. I review the sites listed on the history screen. Surely she can't think I'm a hermaphrodite—she's my mother, she's seen me naked. She must think I'm bisexual. I wonder briefly if there's any advantage in letting her think this, anything I might be able to use to get my own horse. But then I think, gee, this is my mother who knows me better than anyone. Could she be right?

"Mom, do you think I'm bisexual?"

"It doesn't matter what I think," says Mom. "What matters is what you think."

"I don't know what I think."

Mom reaches over and pulls me tight into her. "Sylvie, we will love you no matter what you are. We won't try to change you. You're perfect just the way you are."

I can feel her quivering against me. I hate it when she gets emotional like this. It reminds me of the way she used to be, before she went back to school and became a psychoanalyst. When Uncle Brian died she cried for weeks.

This is such a big deal to her, and I don't get it. Everything has become way too serious and out of proportion. It's time for a joke.

"What if I decide," I start slowly, "that I am . . . ," I pause like Dad would for comedic effect, "an equestrian?"

Mom stiffens against me and then says the scariest thing I've heard all day. "I'll find you a therapist."

First gymnastics, then hi-lights, now this. She's right about one thing: puberty is a very confusing stage, even for someone who isn't there yet.

CHAPTER TWELVE

The therapist says to call him John, not Dr. Clyde, like Mom told me. He works for the same agency as my mom. She's been there almost a year, since she graduated from university. John has been there longer, but Mom says he's younger than her and he's not her boss and he specializes in adolescents. He looks like a sea lion. He's got no neck. I know I'm not supposed to make comments on someone's physical characteristics but John's are kind of hard to miss. And since Mom always says that exercise is an important component of good mental health, I find his condition worrisome. But it also explains to me why Mom has been on a diet ever since she started her job. She says getting overweight is an occupational hazard when you're a therapist and you make your living sitting on your butt listening to people's problems all day. She must have taken one look at John and called Weightwatchers right away.

John has diplomas on one wall and very bad kid art on another. There is one especially pathetic drawing of what is probably meant to be a unicorn: it's something like a horse with four unjointed legs so how it moves I have no idea, and there's a bright yellow spike sticking out of its forehead at an angle that would ensure the poor creature would never be able to graze. Well, maybe in fantasy-land unicorns don't have to eat.

John wants to know what grade I'm in and how I like my teachers and what my favourite subjects are. It's like we're both pretending we don't know why I'm there, but that's okay with me and I relax until he asks if I have any pets.

"Well, yeah, sort of," I say.

"A dog? Cat? Hamster?"

For each one I shake my head. He goes on for a while: rat, iguana, guinea pig, but finally gives up.

"I have barnacles."

"Well that's unusual. More than one? A family?"

I figure he's probably pretending, that Mom has told him about everything, and he's treating me like a dim-wit. I say, "Barnacles are crustaceans. They don't have families." And then because we might as well get down to business I add, "They're hermaphrodites."

"Well who would have thought?"

"With very long penises." This is inappropriate but I want to see how he responds.

He nods thoughtfully. "Well, I guess if you're stuck in one spot . . . ."

I sit back and cross my arms.

"You going to clam up now?" says John.

I look at him blankly.

"That's a joke—you know: barnacles, clams."

"Clams are mollusks, not crustaceans."

"True enough."

I swing my feet under my chair. I don't know what I'm supposed to say now and he's looking at me as though it's my turn.

"So what brings you here?" he asks eventually.

"My mom."

He clears his throat. "Anything I can help you with?"

"I don't think so."

"It's not easy being the kid of a therapist."

"Psychoanalyst," I correct him because Mom has stressed the distinction.

"Even more so."

He probably isn't supposed to say something like this, which makes me like him just a little. "Puberty," I offer.

He purses his lips. "Very difficult stage, from what I hear."

His tone is ironic but I'm not sure if he means he's read about the problems in therapy journals, which would be okay, or if my mom has talked to him about me, which would not be okay.

I sit. He sits. We are both waiting but I know I can outwait anyone. All I have to do is start thinking about horses and I'm off in another world. Kansas has promised me I can start taking lessons on Electra as soon as her riding ring has been built. I told her I thought I'd rather ride Hambone (formerly Nickers) but she didn't think that was a good idea. He's still what she calls an unknown quantity and he's kind of dominant for a gelding and may need a more experienced rider, at least in the beginning. He might be safe after he's been tuned. Obviously I couldn't tell her that I've ridden him already. Electra . . .

"I can help you, Sylvie" says John.

"I don't need any help."

"You've got a problem."

"Not really."

"I think you do."

I don't know if an adolescent expert can look at someone and know that they're bisexual. If he tells me I'm bisexual I'll die. Or I'll leave. I wonder if it's breaking a law to get up and leave in the middle of a therapy session, and whether he can grab me and bring me back in. But even if it isn't illegal, what would my mom say. Would it embarrass her if her daughter was a failure at therapy?

John steeples his fingers and leans way back in his chair. With his weight the chair better be made of specially reinforced materials. "I think your problem is . . . " and he pauses, dropping his head until his lips meet his fingertips, then he whispers, "your mother."

"My mother?"

"If nothing else, your problem is that your mother is worried about you. And I can help you with that. I can help you get her off your back."

Behind John is his desk and on it is a telephone. One of the lights is flashing. He must have the phone on mute so we can't be disturbed. My feet have stopped swinging so I wrap my ankles tight around the chair legs. I don't like it that he's criticized my mom—even if he's right. Electra is quite small, she's only thirteen hands tall. She's chestnut with four white sox and a blaze. Kansas says she's Arab/Welsh and very very smart but that she likes kids, especially light ones like me because she's very fine-boned so she won't give me any trouble and I'll learn a lot from her. And she loves to jump, which I'm not too sure about right now but maybe by the time I—

"I'm thinking we could even do our next session with your mom here. Or better still, with your mom and dad. Generally this is my preference, I tend not to think of problems as being inside people, more I think of them as being between people." He gestures to the middle of the carpet, as though problems could be happening out there in the middle of the room. And I'm not sure how, but I still think he's being critical of my mom. It's like he has a point to make that has nothing to do with me.

How am I going to get out of this? I know what my problem is. My problem is that I want a horse, I've wanted one since I was born and I'm not going to be happy until I have one. But if I tell him that and he thinks the same way Mom does and then wants to talk to me about how a horse is a substitute for conscious masturbation I'll die. I'll crawl under the carpet and die. They'll cart my body out on a stretcher and I will never ride again, let alone have my own horse.

"Well, it's up to you." John shrugs as though it doesn't matter to him, but I know that it does.

I try to picture Hambone but I can't. There's just John, sitting in his over-sized swivel chair, stroking the little bit of beard he has on the place where his chin should be, rocking ever so slightly back and forth. Waiting.

I mumble, "Okay," because this seems to be the only way to get out of the room alive.

"Okay?" He sounds surprised. Or maybe terrifically pleased.

I nod.

"I'll set it up, then," says John. "You, me, Evelyn and your father. It'll be great."

What have I done to my family?

Mom drives me home. She says she doesn't want to be intrusive about the session so she won't ask what we talked about but she does want to know if it went all right. She wants to know what I thought of John. I tell her he was okay. Then I tell her that John is going to talk to her about setting up an appointment for a family session. I think it's better coming from me, then she won't be taken by surprise tomorrow at work.

"A family session?" she says. "He thinks there are problems in the family?"

"He says problems happen between people not inside people."

She sighs. "Well that's one way of looking at things." She isn't pleased.

Mom waits until after dinner before she reminds Dad that I had my appointment today, then she tells him that John wants a family session.

"John?" says Dad. "Wasn't he that cocky little guy at the Christmas party?"

"Well, hardly little," says Mom.

"Short," says Dad, "but . . . "

"Tony," she cautions. "He's Sylvie's therapist."

"Right," says Dad. "But I thought he worked exclusively with kids. I thought he did art therapy and that sort of thing."

"Me too," says Mom. "That's what he used to do. Maybe he's been to a workshop. Maybe he's into family therapy now."

"There's nothing wrong with our family," says Dad. "Is there Snookums?" He puts his arms around me and lifts me right off the ground. He's wearing the aftershave I got him for Christmas and I press my face in hard against his neck.

CHAPTER THIRTEEN

I'm searching for Electra. There is a herd of a hundred chestnut horses with white socks and I can't find her because they all look alike which means I'm a pretty inadequate horse person since I can't tell them apart. I try to remember the particular shape of the blaze on her face and whether it went above her eyes or faded to a snip between her nostrils, but it's no use. And then I see Nickers; she ambles up to me and I'm so happy to see her that I kiss her on the nose, then leap on her back even though there's no saddle, and that's when I realize I must be dreaming and I don't quite manage it right and accidentally wake myself up.

I lie in bed because the alarm won't go off for a few minutes. It's a school day so there's not much to look forward to but Kansas says I can drop by on my way home if I don't have anything else to do, like therapy appointments. She thinks those are funny. She says I'm the most normal kid she's ever met, but I haven't told her everything. I don't want to tell her I might be bisexual in case she worries this means that I might fall in love with her.

Maybe I should have asked John how I can tell if I'm

bisexual or not. Maybe he would have kept it confidential. Or maybe not. My mom says some things that are discussed in therapy cannot be kept confidential because of the law though mostly these things have to do with abuse and self-harm. I don't know how bisexuality fits into that. I don't even really know why I'm thinking about it so much all of a sudden. Unless it's because of the barnacles.

My alarm goes off. I change out of my pajamas then ride my bike to the beach and back. I change the barnacles' water and watch their tentacles for a minute. I still can't see anything that looks like it might be a penis which frankly is a great relief.

Mom and Dad still aren't awake, so I do a few stretches, then put the Pony Club manual on my head and measure myself against the edge of the door. There's been very little progress. To be completely accurate, there's been no progress at all.

At school, we have a substitute teacher for math, which is great because for once I won't have to deal with Mr. Brumby. However the substitute isn't prepared, so she tells us we can read or draw or do whatever we want, so of course everyone goes crazy. I haven't brought a book to read, so I try to drown out the din by drawing, even though I'm lousy at it. My drawings aren't much better than the ones on John's wall, though at least I get the joints in the legs. I know other girls in my class draw horses too and often they end up with prettier art but it's rarely realistic. Or even if they get the horse anatomy fairly accurate, they put the saddles too far back and never put throatlatches on the bridles.

At lunch everyone's still wound up and I know this is exactly the sort of situation where they find someone (like me) to pick on in an extra-merciless way. I decide to avoid the cafeteria altogether, and take my lunch bag to the far corner of the grounds and eat my sandwich sitting under a tree. When I finish, I notice that one of the tree branches is within my reach, so I grab it and have a really good hanging stretch. I hold on a long time until my hands start to ache, and then I close my eyes and hum to distract myself from the pain and extend the stretch as long as possible. When I open my eyes, standing in front of me are Amber and Topaz with three girls from their fan club and Logan Losino. They're not wearing jackets and Amber and Topaz have sleeveless tops on and their bra straps are showing. It's like they think developing breasts is something to brag about and not something personal that should be kept private, which is what I'm going to do if it ever happens to me.

"Hey monkey," says Amber, "did you fall out of your tree?" The girls all giggle.

"Pygmy chimp," says Topaz. Apparently this is hysterically funny.

I don't know what to do. My mom always says to ignore kids like this but if I walk away it will look like they've won and maybe they'll throw a rock at the back of my head. My dad says to fight them with humour. Being under pressure, all I can come up with is a weak joke.

"Better a pygmy chimp than a gorilla," I say and then laugh to show that I'm kidding and that I haven't taken offence because truly I would rather be a pygmy chimp than a gorilla.

"Who you calling a gorilla?" says Amber. She steps menacingly towards me but Logan Losino grabs her arm.

"Oh leave her alone," he says. "She's not hurting anyone."

Amber whirls to face him. "Says who?"

Logan bows his knees and holds his arms out from his sides and hoots. "Says me, and I'm the king of the jungle." He hops up and down, gorilla-like.

Amber laughs and shoves him on the shoulder. He staggers backwards and falls, a bit too easily from what I can see, but everyone is laughing now and trying to pick him up but he keeps hooting and falling and I make my escape. I feel exactly like Tootsie, that poor pony that none of the other horses liked. I wonder if the girls in my class can tell that there's something wrong with me and that's why I'm so unpopular. Maybe I've been wrong blaming the change in my social status on the arrival of the Wonder Twins. Maybe it's the arrival of puberty that's done it and the differences between me and everyone else are finally becoming obvious, or even subconsciously obvious. The only one who hasn't noticed is Logan Losino. I feel a warmth in my chest when I think about the way he came to my rescue. Logan Losino. Maybe he still likes me a little.

The rest of the day drags. I keep an eye on my watch all afternoon. When the bell goes and we're dismissed I'm out the door like a shot, before Amber can set up an ambush. I unchain my bike and pedal off to Kansas.

I'm almost run over by a gravel truck loaded with dirt exiting her driveway. It worries me that the gate is open until I notice the fence is finished so there's a separate paddock beside the driveway. I can't see any horses though. On the other side of the barn an excavator is digging out and leveling off the field where Kansas is going to put the riding arena. There's a huge hole in the field, kind of like a sunken hockey rink.

Kansas is supervising. I've never seen her so happy.

"Hey Sylvia! Look, I'm trading topsoil for footing! Can you believe it? I'm going to save thousands!"

"Oh. Great."

"You know what a good all-weather outdoor riding ring costs? Ten thousand dollars. Mine is going to be half that. Can you believe my luck?"

"Wow."

I guess I don't put enough enthusiasm in my voice because she says, "You okay? Have a bad day?"

I'm afraid to say anything because suddenly I know that if I open my mouth I'll cry.

"Hey, how about you come back to the trailer and help me make a pot of tea? I could use a break, I've been supervising all afternoon."

I leave my bike leaning against the barn. Each of the horses is in a stall and I say hi to Hambone before I follow Kansas around to her little trailer. It's about the size of the entrance hall in our house.

"I inherited this too," says Kansas climbing the metal steps and opening the door. "It was my dad's. When he died I got everything—his travel trailer, his truck, and a whole bunch of money the sneaky old codger had squirreled away. That's how I could afford to buy this place. Well, that and my lifetime savings of two grand."

"You had savings? My dad says that all young people have these days are debts."

"I'll have you know I had savings as well as two horses. Though probably the horses cancel out the savings."

I step inside behind her and she points me to a table with corner bench seats. I slide in. There isn't much room. I have to shove over a basket full of clean, folded laundry.

Kansas fills the kettle and puts it on the stove. She turns on the burner, then peers under the kettle. "Damn. Pilot light's gone out again." She turns off the switch and gets a box of matches from a drawer; she strikes a match, turns the switch, pokes in the match and there's a blue poof as the gas ignites.

She rinses the teapot and throws in two tea bags. "I don't have herbal. Do you drink black tea?"

"Oh sure." This is sort of true. Auntie Sally lets me have black tea. Mom says it's full of stimulants I don't need.

There's a pamphlet on the table in front of me. I don't want to look like I'm being nosey so I read it upside down: *U.S. Dressage Federation Guidelines for Arena Construction.*

From a tiny cupboard over the sink Kansas extracts two mismatched coffee mugs, which she puts on the table. "What do you take in it? Milk? Sugar? Cookies on the side?"

She's better equipped than I imagined she would be. I tell her milk for my tea, and cookies would be good. I'm expecting something nutritious like oatmeal raisin but she produces a pack of digestives and slices open the plastic with a carving knife.

"Don't suppose you know anywhere around here I could get some limestone aggregate?"

My heart races. I remember her telling me in my dream that we all need limestone fortifications. These crossovers from my dreams are exciting but also scary, and I can't talk to her about it because in my dreams she has warned me against making bridges. I have to be careful. If I accidentally conjured up a unicorn here in the daytime I'm sure my head would explode.

"What do you need limestone for?" I ask very quietly. I'm hoping that the word limestone isn't a bridge because she used it first.

"What?" she says, so I repeat myself, but louder this time.

"I need limestone aggregate as a base for my dressage arena," she says.

"Can't you Google it?" I'm looking around her trailer, mostly to be sure a unicorn hasn't popped up anywhere, but also for her computer.

"No room for a computer in here."

"You've got room for a laptop. Or a BlackBerry."

"Actually, Sylvia, I don't believe in computers."

I stare at her. She couldn't have told me anything more shocking. My perfect Kansas. "How do you look things up?"

She points to the pamphlet on the table. "I read. I take out books from the library."

Well, maybe she doesn't understand computers, maybe that's the problem. "The library has computers. Someone could show you how to use them."

"I suppose," she says with bland disinterest. She pulls a phone book out of a thin drawer beside the sink. "Maybe the yellow pages will tell me who has limestone." She flips through some pages. "What do you think I should look under?"

"I don't know. Google always knows. You put in anything and it figures it out for you."

"I guess I'm just a technological dinosaur," says Kansas. She stops leafing. "Here—*Trucking*. Hey, the guy who's taking my topsoil should know. He's bringing pit run to fill up the hole, he'll know where to get limestone for the next layer."

I am trying to imagine a life without computers, where you have to look things up in books and get advice from people you don't know. "You can come and use our computer, Kansas. I can help you look things up."

"Thanks, but that's not necessary. I need to get this ring finished, build my business and start conditioning the horses for the show season. I don't have time to sit in front of a computer."

Of course, without computers I also wouldn't be so confused. I wouldn't have found out about hermaphrodites or bisexuals. "But if you have high-speed you can watch on-line videos of horses for sale. And performances on YouTube."

She shakes her head.

"Or you could write down what you need to know and I could look it up for you and bring you the answers."

The kettle whistles and Kansas fills the teapot. Steam covers the inside of the windows of the trailer. She doesn't wait for the tea to steep, like Auntie Sally does. Kansas stirs the teabags around in the pot with a spoon, then squeezes the bags against the sides, pushing out all the caffeine and tannic acid. "Come on," she says, filling the mugs. "Let's take our tea outside and watch what those guys are up to."

But by the time we leave the trailer the guys have shut down their equipment and gone home. The excavator sits in the middle of the hole in the ground looking like a big dead insect.

Kansas balances her mug of tea on top of a pile of dirt and hops down into the hole. There's some water seeping in from the walls. I don't want to follow her because I'll get my shoes too muddy. Kansas is having a great time in her rubber boots. She runs over to the excavator and climbs in the cab and wiggles the control levers. She yells back to me, "I've always wanted to drive one of these!" She's like a big kid.

I stand and sip my tea until she clambers back up out of the hole beside me.

"Let's go put the horses out, they've been in their stalls all day," she says.

I want to put a halter on Hambone but Kansas won't let me.

"You can take Electra. I'm still working on some dominance issues with old Hambone. He thinks he's the herd leader. Actually he's more like a dictator."

"I thought stallions led herds."

She cups a hand beside her mouth away from Hambone and whispers to me, "He thinks he's still a stallion. Probably he never saw the post-surgical report after he was gelded."

"Oh." But I'm thinking, I rode a horse that thinks he's a stallion? My knees get weak and wobbly but Kansas doesn't notice.

"Actually, in the wild many stallions aren't herd leaders the way that Hambone tries to be. Often it's a boss mare who's in charge of finding food and water. The stallion is there to protect the mares from predators—and from other stallions of course. What's interesting to me is that when a mare's in charge of a herd the horses spend more time grazing and relaxing."

Kansas enjoys sharing her horse knowledge with me; her voice gets all perky. It's different than when Mom tries to teach me about life and psychology, partly because I'm truly interested in horses but also because with Mom there's this heavy seriousness that isn't there with Kansas. I trust Kansas completely. I could tell her anything.

But then I realize that of course I haven't told her everything.

We put out Electra and Photon and then Kansas goes back for Hambone, who is kicking the heck out of the back wall of his stall. Kansas stands in front of his door with her arms folded. "You stop that and I'll let you out."

Hambone kicks the wall again and Kansas takes a step backwards away from him. He stares at her, then walks to his stall door and hangs his head out.

"Okay then," says Kansas. She puts a halter on him, clips on the lead rope and before she takes him out she tells me to stay well out of the way. But he walks like a perfect gentleman out to the paddock and it's not until she's slipped off the halter and set him free that he flattens his ears, spins and takes off screaming after his mares, driving them to the far end of the pasture, all of them bucking and kicking and striking like maniacs.

"Don't they mind being treated that way? Electra and Photon, I mean."

Kansas shrugs. "It's herd dynamics."

Hambone bites Photon on the bum and a chunk of fur

flies into the air. She squeals and kicks and he bites her again. Kansas laughs and shakes her head. "He is such a moron. When Electra and Photon were together at my last place, Electra was boss mare, and she could move Photon across the pasture with the flick of an ear. Hambone goes way overboard. Makes me wonder if he's not proudcut."

"Proudcut?"

"Well the technical term is *crypt orchid*. In some stallions only one testicle drops and when they are gelded the other testicle is left up inside them. So—*crypt*, as in hidden, and *orchid* for testicle."

I think I am never going to know all the gender variations that nature has to offer. It seems that so many things can go wrong, it's something of a miracle if everything turns out the way we think it's supposed to.

The mares want to graze; they stop, lower their heads and grab a bit of grass, but Hambone isn't finished yet. He runs at them with ears pinned, rears, then pushes them down the fence line.

"How'd you like to ride that?" says Kansas, following Hambone's trajectory with her eyes.

I lean on the fence beside her and take a deep breath. She might as well know. "Well, actually, I have ridden him."

"You have?" She's not mad like my mom would be. She's more just surprised.

"Before you got here. I put my skipping rope around his neck and rode him in the field. Not very much. It was too scary."

"No kidding." Now she sounds impressed.

"He didn't want to go. But he understood English, so when I figured that out he did what I asked him."

"Well I'll be damned. There's more hope for that horse than I thought. And you!" She puts a gloved hand on my shoulder and looks at me with admiration. "Well you're full of surprises too!"

"I wore my bike helmet."

"Well that's good. But you have to promise me that you won't do it again."

I shake my head. "No way. Not now that I've seen what he can be like."

"Hey," says Kansas looking around. "Where's my tea?" She spies it on the dirt pile and strolls over to retrieve it. A swell of warmth comes over me as I watch her, realizing how she didn't make a big deal of my riding Hambone without permission. Mom would have turned it into a two-hour safety lecture.

Kansas comes back to the fence and drinks down her tea in a couple of gulps. It can't be very hot. She wipes her lips on the back of her sleeve, then pulls a pack of cigarettes out of her jacket pocket. I couldn't be more shocked if she'd grown horns, sprouted wings and flown away. This is even less understandable than her not wanting to use computers.

"You smoke?"

"Not often." She flicks a lighter and draws on the cigarette.

"But cigarettes cause cancer. Everyone knows that."

"I'm working on it."

"My Uncle Brian used to smoke. My mom told him he had to quit, and he did, but it was too late and he died anyway." This is only partly true, because it's never been totally clear to me that Uncle Brian died from smoking, but I'm desperate. I can't take a chance on Kansas dying of lung cancer.

"Well, I'm sorry to hear that," says Kansas.

"Maybe I could help you quit, maybe if I reminded you . . . "

Kansas shakes her head, then takes a drag on her cigarette. She turns her face away and blows a thin stream of smoke into the paddock. "Thanks, Sylvia, but I don't expect that would work very well. I'm a boss mare kind of person. No one's ever been any good at telling me to do anything."

I try to smile at her. I try to think of something else that might change her mind. I tell myself it's none of my business but then I'm overwhelmed with this horrible sense of helplessness as I see how little control I have of my life and of anyone else's life, how I can't make bad people stop doing mean things and I can't make good people stop doing dumb things and it's so hard to be fourteen and I can't imagine fifteen being much better and a huge lump forms in my throat and my eyes fill with tears and a ridiculous embarrassing sobbing noise erupts from my chest.

"Hey," says Kansas.

And she looks at me and I don't even cover my face with my hands, the tears stream out of me as I stand there like an idiot.

"Hey, okay, I'll put it out. I was going to quit anyway, one day. Why not now?"

CHAPTER FOURTEEN

That night after dinner we have one of our dreaded family conferences because Mom and Dad can't agree on whether to go to a family therapy session with John and they want my "input".

Dad says he doesn't like John, and Mom says that doesn't mean he isn't a good therapist. Dad says we should be seeing someone from outside of Mom's agency and Mom says she wouldn't know who to pick because every day she sees a new refugee from another counselling practice. Dad says that of course all she hears are bad stories because if someone is happy with their therapist they never leave them or better still they are cured and don't need to go see someone else. Mom says Dad is frightened and there's nothing to be frightened of because we have a good family and Dad says in that case why do we need to go? At which point they both look at me.

"I'm fine," I say.

They look at me some more.

"I don't need a therapist. I have you to talk to—both of you."

"What if there was something you didn't want to talk about with your parents?" says Mom. "Something about boys or—"

Before she can add anything more embarrassing I say, "I could talk to my friends."

There's a long silence and my mom says, "What friends, Pumpkin?"

"Kansas."

They look at each other.

"Who's Kansas?" says Dad.

"My new friend."

"Is Kansas a . . . a . . . boy?" says Dad.

My nose wrinkles. "No," I say, bewildered. Why would I want a boy friend? Boys aren't interested in horses.

"Is this someone new in your class?" says Mom. "Because we haven't heard about her before."

I don't want to tell them, but it has to come out sooner or later. I try to tell them carefully so they don't find reasons for objecting to my friendship with Kansas. I don't tell them that she used to smoke cigarettes, or that her clothing looks second-hand, or that she lives in a trailer behind a barn. "She's really nice. She says she'll give me riding lessons if I help out at her stable. She's on the way to school."

"And how old is this person?" says Dad.

I have no idea. Who cares? She likes horses. She owns horses. She treats me like a human being. She could be fifty and I wouldn't care. "I'll ask her."

"Is she married?" says Mom.

The two of them are relentless. "No."

Dad is looking at Mom with alarm. "You don't suppose she could be a lesbian? Preying on little girls?"

I can't believe he said this. It is so insulting. Placing slow, venomous emphasis on every word, I say, "I am not a little girl."

"Oh, Tony, for heaven's sake," says Mom. I'm glad to see that she's angry too. "How many times do we have to go through this? *Gay* does not mean *pedophile*. My brother Brian—"

She stops. Her face is turning red. Is she going to cry?

"Kansas is not a lesbian," I say, using my most exasperated tone. Of course, I don't know if Kansas is a lesbian but at this point I don't care. And what would it matter anyway? Maybe it would be better if she was a lesbian since I'm probably a bisexual but I don't know and I don't care and it doesn't matter. She likes horses.

"Does she have family in town?" says Dad.

Mom sniffs. "Could we meet her at least?"

"You two are piling on," I say.

"We are not," they say together.

I fold my arms. I am not going to answer another question.

"I really think we should meet her," says Mom.

I tighten my lips. I don't want them to meet her. She's my friend.

"Okay, that settles it," says Mom.

"Fine, but not John," says Dad.

"I'll find someone else. I've heard there's a new therapist in town with a special interest in adolescent sexuality."

I groan aloud. My life is ruined. All the limestone fortification in the world couldn't save me now.

I am banned from the computer until I get some therapy. I think this goes way beyond punishment, and infringes on my human rights. Computers aren't toys. The internet is more than a source of mindless passive entertainment like cable TV. My parents are depriving me of an education and they are isolating me from the Googleverse. I think about reporting them to the Helpline for children but I know they will also be monitoring my telephone calls so there's no point in trying. I am totally at their mercy—it always comes down to this.

The situation is so hopeless that I shut myself in my room and do something truly desperate. I sit on my bed and cross my legs and close my eyes and try to imagine being surrounded by white light and being protected by a white unicorn with a golden horn, like Taylor does. Nothing happens. I think maybe my position isn't right so I sit in the chair at my desk and try again, but still nothing happens. Taylor seemed to think this was easy, but she has more experience being spiritual than I do. The only other spiritual position I know is what people do when they pray, so I kneel beside my bed, put my hands together, bow my head and close my eyes. That's when Dad comes in.

"Jesus," he says.

I open my eyes and look at him but I don't get off my knees.

"What are you doing, Munchkin?"

I'm so mad at him that I say what I know will really bother him. "I'm praying."

Dad comes in, shuts the door behind him and sits on my bed. "When did you get religious? Is this something you got from your new friend?" He makes it sound like a disease that I could accidentally catch from somebody. Obviously if there's to be any possibility of retaining my friendship with Kansas I have to keep her well out of this.

"Taylor taught me."

"Your cousin Taylor? She's a Christian?"

Still I'm not sure how far to take things. "I think she's more of a Druid."

He relaxes a little. "Oh. Well, I'm still a bit surprised . . . "

"You're the ones who named me after an ancient nature goddess."

"Sylvia? That's what it means?"

I am so smitten by hearing my full name roll off his tongue that all I can manage is one brief nod.

He ruffles my hair, then says he didn't mean to mess up the hi-lights, which makes me laugh so I get up off my knees and sit beside him on the bed. He puts his arm around me and I start to cry. Again. I hate this so much.

"I said I was sorry," says Dad.

I grab my head in both hands and groan. "I don't care about the hi-lights," I yell at him. "I only did it for Mom and because she said you would like it."

"Well I do like it, Shorty," he says and gives me a squeeze.

And I'm drawing my breath to tell him to stop calling me Shorty when the door opens and Mom pops her head in and says, "You two doing okay?"

"We're doing fine, Evelyn. Aren't we, Munchkin?" He squeezes me again. I feel like a tube of toothpaste. If he squeezes me much more there's no telling what might come out. I am really really mad at both of them. I close my eyes. I'm trying to control myself. The bed sags as Mom sits down, then she wiggles up against me. She tries to put an arm around me but it's difficult because Dad is holding me tight under his armpit and there's no room for Mom's hand and he's not giving way. I feel her fingers scrabbling against my ribs. I can't make space for her because Dad will feel me moving away from him towards Mom, and I can't stay like this or Mom will think I don't want her here. I scrunch my eyelids tighter together and try to close my ears too because I really don't want to hear them if they start going at each other, and that's when the white light happens. It starts as this tiny white speck and it grows and grows until I'm breathing it in and breathing it out and it must be filling the whole room but I'm not going to take the chance of opening my eyes and ruining anything. There's a hum in the distance which is probably the voices of my mom and dad but they're so far away it doesn't matter. I'm okay. I am really okay.

And I hear a funny rippling sound, kind of like neighing, kind of like laughing.

It's the unicorn.

CHAPTER FIFTEEN

There are no horses, but somehow I know I'm dreaming. I'm in the middle of a big field of tall grass with flowers growing in it—blue ones and white ones that look like daisies—but I sniff one and it's stinky. I wonder why there are no horses, and then I figure since it's a dream and it's my dream and it's a lucid dream why don't I put into it whatever I want? And don't ask me why, but I try for a unicorn. Maybe I don't want to take a chance on disappointing Kansas again by saying the wrong thing, and maybe I'm tired of trying to figure out if it's Nickers or Hambone or Prince Hamlet and I'm not sure about riding him anyway if he's got dominance issues. But right away there's a unicorn beside me, not very big, just pony sized which is perfect really because I can put my arm across his back and walk around with him that way. When he turns his head sideways I can see a horn, not a silly long golden one that would get in the way of grazing or self-grooming, but a sensible, short white horn.

"I'm glad you're not trying to ride me," says the unicorn. His lips move when he talks.

"Well I guess not," I say. "That would be undignified."

"It certainly would. But that doesn't stop some nitwits from trying."

He's sounding pretty self-assured, maybe even dominant, which gets me wondering if he's a he or a she, so I stop and I'm about to bend down and have a look up under the unicorn's belly when he or she says, "Please—don't even think about it. Those are my private parts. Private," he or she stresses.

"Okay."

We resume our stroll.

"I thought you were imaginary," I say.

"Whatever."

"You don't care?"

"Doesn't make any difference to me what you believe."

This is a surprise. Somehow I'd expected more of an effort to convert me. Everyone else seems to be trying.

"Good," I say.

"It's not as though I spend any time believing in you or caring what you think."

Which is such a twisted thought that of course I wake up.

I lie in bed thinking about how much I care about what other people think. It's lots. Obviously I care what my parents think because I want them to be happy with me and not worry about me too much. And I worry about what the kids at school think of me and wonder why they don't like me, except possibly for Logan Losino. And there are my cousins who think I'm some sort of idiot. And I really, really want Kansas to like me. Maybe my whole life is taken up with thinking about what other people think. I wonder what it would be like to be a unicorn and not think about this stuff at all. What would he do instead—just think about himself? Then it occurs to me that maybe there isn't much difference between these two options. Whether I thought about myself all the time or thought about what other people were thinking about me, when it comes right down to it, it's all thinking about me. There has to be more to life than this. I get up, dress and ride down to the beach for a fresh supply of sea water for the barnacles.

Over breakfast I learn that Dad will be driving me to school and picking me up in the afternoon. Until I'm back on track, Mom says. Meaning until I've been to see a therapist and am cured of whatever is wrong with me. Also meaning they don't want me to see Kansas.

Of course, Dad forgets to pick me up after school. I sit on the steps and wait for him until four o'clock, which is long enough for everyone in the school to walk past and tease me.

"Hey, Monkey, did you lose your bike in the jungle?" says Amber.

"Oops, sorry Pygmy, didn't see you sitting there, you're so SMALL," says Topaz.

Even after they're halfway down the sidewalk they're still talking about me and laughing. "Have you seen her midget fingernails? They look like claws! And then there's her ears!"

I drop my head so my hair falls around my ears in a shield; I hope I don't hear any more but I do.

"Little monkey ears. Do you think she could actually be part monkey?"

I want to hide somewhere but can't leave in case I miss Dad.

The only one who's sort of nice to me is Logan Losino. He walks past, then comes back and stands at the bottom of the stairs. He pulls a pack of gum out of his back pocket and offers me a foil-wrapped stick. Then he leaves without saying a word. Now what does that mean?

Finally Dad pulls up and honks the horn. He's all flustered and suggests we not tell Mom and he promises he won't be late tomorrow. He offers to stop at the beach for some sea water but of course I don't need that, I got it already this morning. But he's still looking for a way to make it up to me, so he says, "How about we drive home past your friend Dakota's house?"

"Her name is Kansas. And I don't want to."

It doesn't matter, he's going to do it anyway.

"Must be this way," he says, turning off the main road. And somehow he finds the right street, without any help from me. I guess it's not too difficult, there isn't that much farmland within biking distance of our house. My plan is to sink down in my seat and not let him know when we're going by Kansas's driveway, but I'm also pretty curious about what progress has been made, so I sit up as long as I can. We reach the edge of Kansas's property and I can see the barn in the distance, and a gravel truck unloading in her ring, when Dad stops the car at the side of the road and says, "Is that her?"

I look to the back of the field, and there's Kansas riding Hambone. They're doing little figure-eights at the canter and on the third one when they cross the center part Hambone bunches up and does a huge buck.

"Boy, she can really ride," says Dad.

I'm not even watching Kansas. My eyes are glued on Hambone who has turned into a bucking bronco. He must buck five more times before Kansas gets him going forward in a big circle.

I rode that horse—bareback with a skipping rope around his neck, and he did everything that I asked him without the smallest buck. He must really like me. Or I was really lucky.

Kansas is now trotting Hambone up the fence line away from us.

Dad puts on the turn signal and pulls back onto the road.

"Doesn't look very safe," he says.

I peer out my side window, in the opposite direction from Kansas. Maybe I can pretend I didn't see anything. In any event I'm not going to speak. In particular, I'm not going to say anything critical about Kansas. There's nothing interesting out this side so I slouch down against the door and stare straight ahead at the glove box. This must be what my barnacles feel like, tucked inside strong walls . . . being taken places they don't want to go. Dad turns on the radio. It's tuned to a classical music station that is even more boring than school.

CHAPTER SIXTEEN

I decide to set my barnacles free. It doesn't seem fair that I have them in captivity only so I can make a point with my parents. I know I'm taking good care of them, but it won't be the same for them as living wild in the ocean. And besides, my plan doesn't seem to be working.

So when we get home, Dad says he has to make some phone calls and I tell him I'm going to the beach. I'm not sure if he heard me so I also leave a note on the table in case Mom comes home before I return. I wrap my barnacles in a towel, stuff them in my pack and take them back where I got them.

There's no one else on the beach and fortunately the tide is out. I prop my bike against a log, then scramble down to the tide pools where the barnacles grow. I can't remember which exact pool I took my barnacles from and hope it doesn't matter to them because wherever I put them, they're stuck there for the rest of their lives. I put them in one pool, then change my mind and put them in another one. I'm still not sure, but then I think anything is going to be better than living in a Pyrex dish in my bedroom in support of a lost cause.

I sit on a rock and watch them until they start waving their little arms around collecting food, or maybe they're waving goodbye to me. Goodbye and good riddance they'll be thinking.

At least they have their own personal little limestone castles to live in. They have that advantage over me.

While I'm pedaling home I prepare for the lecture I'm bound to receive about how easily I changed my mind and how pets require a long-term commitment and maybe I should trust my parents' judgment when they say I'm not ready for something.

But no one notices—which is good and bad at the same time. It's good that I won't be lectured, but bad because they probably never really noticed that I did a responsible job in the first place. So I'm no further ahead.

At dinner Mom announces that she has good news. She's found an adolescent psychiatrist with an excellent reputation and normally there's a six-month waiting list but he will see me soon because Mom is sort of a colleague, or at least she works in the same general field, or maybe because her boss phoned and asked. And I'm thinking that's great, everyone in her office must know now.

"A psychiatrist?" says Dad. He looks shocked, and for a second I think I'm saved, that he will say I don't need to see a psychiatrist, that I'm not crazy, that really there's nothing wrong with me. But instead he says, "I won't need to go, will I? We won't be doing family therapy with a psychiatrist will we?"

"Oh, I don't think so," says Mom. "Not for the first session, anyway. I'll take her." She turns to me. "He's supposed to be really nice. Everyone likes him."

And I'm thinking, Not me. I won't like him.

And Dad says, "Well at least a psychiatrist will be covered by our medical insurance. Your friend John was very expensive."

Mom looks a bit stunned. "He charges the same as I do."

Dad shrugs. "Still expensive."

Mom sighs. "We'll need a referral from our family doctor before we can see a specialist, so I'll have to set up an appointment with Dr. Destrie first."

"Oh no," I say. "I don't like Dr. Destrie."

"Hasn't he retired yet?" says Dad.

"I hope not," says Mom. "He's been my doctor for as long as I can remember."

"My point exactly," says Dad.

"Which makes him very experienced," says Mom.

"More like stuck in his ways," says Dad.

And off they go. I excuse myself from the table and go to my room to work on my math. If I re-read it often enough I figure eventually it has to sink in.

At 7:30 I hear the phone ringing and a minute later Mom is tapping at my door saying it's for me. No one phones me. What's even more of a surprise is that Mom hands me the cordless then closes the door so I can talk in privacy.

But it's only Taylor.

"I thought I should warn you that Stephanie is on the warpath," she says.

"I didn't do anything," I say automatically.

"Your mom told my mom that you said that Stephanie was telling you all about bisexuality. What were you thinking?"

I feel sick. I don't need Stephanie against me along with everyone else. She will be merciless. She's mean enough when she likes you. But how to explain what happened? I hardly know myself.

"There was a misunderstanding," I begin.

"I'll say," says Taylor. "Your mom told my mom that she thinks Stephanie was being highly inappropriate in discussing sexuality with someone your age."

"But I didn't say anything about that. And Mom talks to me about sexuality all the time."

Taylor is enjoying her reporter role so she doesn't listen. "So my mom defended Stephanie of course and then my mom and your mom had an argument about parenting skills, but afterwards my mom phoned Stephanie and accused her anyway and of course Stephanie denied everything but then Stephanie always denies everything so Mom didn't believe her."

"That's not my fault."

"Of course it's your fault. And you have to take responsibility for it."

This is too much, receiving instruction like this from Taylor. "You're not sounding very spiritual right now, Taylor."

I can hear static on the line because it's an old cordless phone. Mom wants us to buy a new one but Dad says it's perfectly good and we're not replacing it until it dies—just like Mom's car.

Eventually Taylor says, "You're right."

I hear her take some deep calming breaths.

So I tell her exactly what happened, about the trail I accidentally left on the history file of the web browser, and how guilty I'd been feeling about sneaky guerilla marketing so I confessed to this instead of to looking at the bisexuality sites which was what Mom was upset about. And how I'd implicated Stephanie about the marketing plan, but not the other stuff. And how Mom had got it all mixed up and now thought that I was bisexual.

"God, you're hardly unisexual let alone bisexual," says Taylor.

"I'm a late-bloomer."

"If you say so."

"Everything's a mess. My mom wants me to see an adolescent psychiatrist."

"Oh, lucky you," says Taylor. At first I think she's being sarcastic like Stephanie, but then she says, "There's only one in town and I hear he's super cute. A friend of mine sees him."

I don't care if he's cute but of course I don't tell Taylor that. She and her sisters already think I'm weird enough. "I have to see Dr. Destrie first for a referral."

"Ewww. Not Dr. Destrie. I thought he retired. We haven't used him since he gave Stephanie cortisone cream for what he thought was a fabric softener allergy and actually she had chlamydia."

I don't know what clamidia is, but I don't want to ask— she already thinks I'm a moron. Maybe it's a sea food allergy, but I would have thought even Dr. Destrie could tell the difference between that and a skin reaction to fabric softener.

"My mom's still a big fan of Dr. Destrie," I say.

"Well if it's only for a referral maybe he won't have to examine you. As long as he doesn't have to touch you it won't be too bad. And I'll try to sort things out with Stephanie for you."

There's another long silence. I don't know what Taylor is thinking, but I'm imagining being examined by Dr. Destrie. I don't mind him looking down my throat or in my ears, but probably to sort out this bisexuality question he's going to be looking somewhere else. I don't think I could stand that.

"There's one more thing," Taylor says.

From the way she's hesitating I figure she's saved the worst news for last. I already feel like a crumpled sock in the bottom of the laundry hamper, what with Stephanie out to get me and Dr. Destrie about to examine me. It's difficult to imagine what could be worse. "What," I say flatly, totally defeated already.

"I'm supposed to be trying to talk you into taking ballet lessons. Your mom asked my mom."

"But I don't like ballet."

"They seem to think you don't have enough hobbies or positive influences in your life."

"Not ballet."

"I told them I'd try. I'm supposed to mention that it will make you taller."

I look around my empty room. No barnacles. No computer. There is the Pony Club manual and the Greenhawk Equestrian Supplies catalogue. If I opened the door I would see the purple mark a foot over my head.

"I'll think about it," I say. Maybe I could use this as a negotiating tool to get out of seeing a psychiatrist.

CHAPTER SEVENTEEN

I'm walking across a meadow with the unicorn. I think we're walking to the psychiatrist's office, but I'm not sure why. Whatever we're doing, I'm not very happy about it. I'm about to ask the unicorn what his/her name is when it says, "You did the right thing about the barnacles. I know it was difficult—often the right thing is."

"Thanks." I'm glad that someone has noticed. This helps me feel less sad.

"But forget about naming me."

"Okay."

"And if you had some gender-free way of referring to me, that would be good, but since I'm not fond of the pronoun it, you may use the male words."

"Okay." I look down. I'm wearing a pink leotard with some frilly netting around my waist. On my feet are pink satin slippers with pink ribbons that wind up around my calves.

The unicorn stops, turns his head and takes a long hard look at me. His horn seems shorter but before I can ask about it he says, "You look . . . " He seems unable to find the right word.

"Stupid?"

"Worse. You look kind of dead. All your shine has gone. And all those lights you get around your head when you're with the hornless ones have disappeared."

My hand goes automatically to my hair—could the hi-lights have faded?

"No, not that, not the colours you put in your mane."

Not that I would have cared. Those hi-lights have only got me unwanted attention. "Hornless ones? Do you mean horses?"

"Use the abbreviated term if you must."

We plod on.

"I feel like there's something wrong with me."

The unicorn grunts.

"My mom says everyone feels like there's something wrong with them which is why we have to work on our self-esteem all the time."

"Yeah, I've heard that one," says the unicorn. "The difference here is that there really is something wrong with you."

I stop in my tracks. The unicorn keeps walking.

"I thought you were spiritual and would protect me and lift me up."

"Well sure," he says over his shoulder. "But there's still reality."

"Reality? You're a unicorn! You're mythical!"

He turns on his haunches until he faces me, executing a perfect walk-pirouette, like the ones I've seen on dressage videos on YouTube. His back feet keep moving up and down in one place and his front feet follow an arc. If he'd been in a competition he would have got a ten out of ten.

"We're not talking about me," says the unicorn. "We're talking about you, and you are real."

"And there's something wrong with me?"

"Unfortunately, yes."

"Not just that I'm unique?"

"Unfortunately not. Don't pretend that you're surprised."

Well I'm not. And it's such a fantastic relief to be talking about it and not talking about vague things like low self-esteem that I smile so hard I wake myself up.

I check my clock and there's still ten minutes before my alarm goes off. And I don't have to make the trip to the beach for seawater any more, so I've got some time to myself to think.

Sure, it was only a dream, but somehow it makes sense. There's something wrong with me. And I don't think it's that I'm bisexual, because technically that's not wrong.

I climb out of bed then lie back down on the floor and do some stretching exercises. I wonder if I should be scared, and at first I'm not. After all, the unicorn didn't tell me to get to a hospital right away because I was going to die. He didn't say I was an alien and would explode soon. So I'm okay, but I'm not, which is very confusing, not to mention weird. The more I think about it the worse I feel. The kids at school are right. I'm a freak. Or maybe I'm broken in some way, maybe I need a repair job, like how Stephanie had her nose fixed. I wish I'd had the sense to ask the unicorn whether there was a possibility of repair and who should be doing it. I don't know what to do.

I'm lying stiff on the floor. I must have stopped doing stretching exercises several minutes ago. There are goose bumps on my arms, only partly from being cold. Mostly I have them because I'm so frightened.

It seems I only have one option, and I hate it. But it looks like I'm going to have to enlist the assistance of my parents.

❄

I know I can't eat any breakfast. I'm sure if I try to swallow something it will only come right back up again. So I play with my porridge. The beach of golden sand dissolves before my eyes, and the island sinks under the pool of milk.

Eventually the stock report on the radio comes to an end. Before Dad can push his chair back, I say, "I think there's something wrong with me."

"Oh, Honey," says Mom.

"There's nothing wrong with my little ray of sunshine!" says Dad.

"No, I mean really," I say.

"Are you feeling okay? You haven't eaten. Do you have the flu? Do you need to stay home from school?" Mom is patting my face feeling for a temperature.

"It's not that."

Mom pushes up my sleeve and feels for a pulse. "A bit fast," she says. "Are you anxious about something? Is this about what we've been talking about? Because being bisexual is not wrong, Cupcake. But if you're feeling it's wrong then that's why you need to talk to the psychiatrist."

Dad gets up from the table and puts his dishes in the washer.

"Tony, you should be part of this," says Mom.

Dad sits back down but he doesn't look at me, which is fine because Mom is looking at me hard enough for both of them.

"Never mind," I say. This was not a good idea. I should have known better. They're making everything worse.

"You're fine," says Mom. "It's normal to feel like an outsider sometimes, to feel different. Right, Tony?"

"Oh sure," says Dad.

"Okay, I understand," I say, hoping it doesn't sound like I'm caving too quickly.

"And no matter what, we love you very much, don't we, Tony?"

"We sure do, Munchkin," says Dad.

"That's good then," I say. I make a show of checking my watch. "Hey, it's time for school. Are you driving me, Dad?"

They both check their watches and we're off in a flurry, like someone has opened a cage and we've all burst free.

Mom is waiting for me in the parking lot after school. She's made an appointment for me with Dr. Destrie. Oh lucky day. It takes ten minutes to re-start the car and we're late for the appointment but we still have to sit for half an hour in his waiting room. I read old *Reader's Digest* magazines because I'm trying not to think about being examined and because I like the jokes; I read the good ones to Mom but she's not interested. She's flipping through *Psychology Today* magazine, sighing a lot and complaining about their "biological approach to mental health".

Finally the receptionist calls my name. Mom comes in with me and we sit for another ten minutes in an examination room. We forgot to bring our magazines. There's a big window with slatted blinds that are half-open. If I stretch up tall I can see out into the parking lot, but if I slouch down I can't. I do this a few times, changing the angle at which I'm looking through the curtains, because I need to figure out whether someone outside in the parking lot could look through the slats and see me naked if Dr. Destrie has to examine me. The examination table is against the wall beside the window. A long strip of white paper runs down the middle of the table. There are metal handles at one end that look like torture devices.

"Sylvie, sit still."

"Mom, what are those called?" I point to the handles at the end of the table.

"They're stirrups, Honey."

"Well that's stupid. Are you teasing me? How can you have stirrups without a saddle?"

"Oh, Sylvie. Please sit still and wait. Everything will be fine."

Mom is fidgeting more than I am—plus even when she's not talking to me she's moving her lips. I guess she's rehearsing what she wants to say. She's always nervous dealing with Dr. Destrie even though she's known him since the last century, but now she says she's extra nervous because not only is he an authority figure, he's also a colleague so she has to negotiate a new relationship with him. Well, whatever she comes up with is fine with me, she can do all the talking because I sure don't know what to say. I could tell him I miss my barnacles. I could tell him I'm picked on at school and my only friend, other than possibly Logan Losino, is Kansas and my parents won't let me see her because they're afraid she's a predatory lesbian when really she's this amazing equestrian. I could tell him I need to grow faster. I could tell him I want a horse.

Dr. Destrie comes in and closes the door behind him. He shakes Mom's hand. "Good to see you, Evelyn," he says, then he ruffles my hair like I'm a five-year-old or a golden retriever. "Hey, Erika."

"Erika is my cousin. I'm Sylvia."

"You're thinking of Sally's youngest," Mom says, smiling.

"So what's the problem here, Sal?" says Dr. Destrie turning to me. I'm sure he said Sal. It could have been Syl but that wouldn't have been much better.

"Sylvie," says Mom, heavily emphasizing the first syllable, "is having some problems related to puberty and we would like a referral to see Dr. Gelderlander, the adolescent psychiatrist." My mom sounds like such a dork. Sometimes I think I liked her better before she learned to be a helping professional even if she was crying half the time.

Dr. Destrie flops into his swivel chair. He tilts way back and laughs. "Oh come on, Evelyn. A psychiatrist? All kids need is a good grandmother. Isn't that right, Syl?"

Mom clears her throat three times. I can't imagine what she's got caught in there.

"Both my grandmothers are dead," I say. This would probably be a good opportunity to tell him about my grandfather and what he's promised me and how that would change my life because finally, I would have the horse that I've wanted forever, but somehow I can't manage it. I don't trust this guy.

"Ahh," says Dr. Destrie. He smiles at me. He doesn't have good teeth. They're yellow and bent over top of each other as though he grew too many for the size of his mouth. I guess they hadn't invented orthodontics when he was a child. "Why don't you tell me what's bothering you?"

"There's nothing bothering me." I'd rather let the guy physically examine me than tell him anything personal about my life.

"Honey, this morning at breakfast you thought there was something wrong with you," says Mom, able to speak at last.

"I made a mistake."

We sit quietly, Dr. Destrie with what's probably supposed to be a look of friendly grandmotherly concern on his face, my mom with her lips pressed out like she's about to spit sunflower seeds, and me trying to look happy and normal.

Finally Mom says, "Peaches, how about you go back to the waiting room and I'll talk to Dr. Destrie for a minute."

Peaches? That's a new one, and somehow it's worse than all the others. Soft sweet pastel-coloured fruit. I slide slowly out of my chair, wondering what I could possibly do to save myself, because I know what Mom's going to say after I leave: that I'm obsessed with getting taller and I want to kill her and marry my father and I can't even be trusted to take care of a dish of barnacles without losing interest. I scuff across the room and stop with my hand on the door knob. I look at my mom, who is smiling at me as though she's completely harmless and has only my best interests at heart and I tell her, "Don't forget to tell him that you think I'm bisexual." And I go and sit out my defeat in the car.

After dinner Taylor phones me. "Did he examine you?"

"No."

"Oh, thank goodness for that. I was so worried about you."

That's nice to hear. I didn't think anyone was worried about me. Well, Mom's worried, but somehow it doesn't seem to be worry about me exactly. She's worried about being a good parent, or worried about worry. I don't quite understand it. Besides, she's worried all the time so it almost doesn't count if she's a bit worried about me. Taylor is another matter.

"Dr. Destrie wanted me to talk to him, but I wasn't comfortable telling him anything, so I just said nothing was bothering me."

"And you got away with that?"

"Sort of. My mom told me to wait outside while she had a private discussion with him, and he agreed to refer me to Dr. Gelderlander."

"That'll be okay. He's supposed to be fun to talk to. You'll have to wait though, maybe three months."

"My mom says he'll see me faster than that because of professional courtesy."

"I'd love to see Dr. Gelderlander. It would be so interesting talking to a psychiatrist. Not that I need to. It's more Erika who needs to."

"What's wrong with Erika?"

"She's very immature. But that's probably mostly because of how Mom keeps treating her like a baby."

"I don't think I've ever been treated like a baby."

"Well you wouldn't like it after the first five minutes of getting whatever you wanted by throwing a tantrum."

I think about having a tantrum as a way of getting a horse. It doesn't seem like the best way to demonstrate maturity and responsibility. Plus, I don't know how I could live with myself. Still, the notion of negotiating for what I want is intriguing. "So Erika gets her way by acting like a baby, and Stephanie gets her way by acting like . . . ." I can't think of the right word to describe her.

"By acting like Stephanie," says Taylor.

"Maybe it's not so bad being an only child," I say, imagining the perpetual uproar in that house, which leaves Taylor to slide around unnoticed under the radar of a worn-down parent. "So how do you get your way?"

Taylor is silent for a moment. "Well I concentrate my mind on what I want, and have positive thoughts about it, so if it's meant to be it will happen."

"That's it? Is that how you got your ballet lessons?"

"I just asked. Mom said she didn't have the money but she'd ask Grandpa and of course he said fine. Then I had to promise that I would practice and commit myself for a whole year but of course that was unnecessary, I knew I'd love ballet."

"But what if there was something big that you wanted . . . "

"Like a horse for example."

"Right. And you had positive thoughts about it for a long, long time, years even, and you asked your mom and she said no but you still really wanted it more than anything in the world and you had a place to keep it that wouldn't be expensive because you could work there, and you had someone to buy it, so all you really need is permission. Well, and some tack. What would you do?"

"I guess I'd keep the pressure on, gently, all the time. I'd keep talking about it. And probably I would pray."

"I don't think I'm spiritual enough for that. Plus I think Dad doesn't approve of prayer."

"Well I guess you could always play the guilt angle somehow—that's what Stephanie did. She whined about being separated from her friends last time we moved and Mom was so worried about her fitting into a new social group that she asked Grandpa to pay for the plastic surgery on her nose."

"That won't work for me—we haven't moved. And I don't want to move." I wouldn't mind changing schools but the thought of living farther away from Kansas is intolerable.

"Maybe you could get your parents to break up—divorce creates lots of guilt."

"Very funny."

"Stephanie thinks she's the reason my mom and dad broke up. I think that's why she's so mean and unhappy and has so many different boyfriends." Taylor is obviously in training to be a therapist, but somehow I don't mind. Instead, I'm suddenly impressed by the amount of thought she has put into other people's lives instead of focusing on her own all the time, like I do.

"I don't want my parents to break up."

"Then you have to find something else for them to feel guilty about. It shouldn't be difficult. Mom says she started feeling guilty the minute Stephanie was born and hasn't stopped since. She says this is normal, so your mom must feel the same way."

I'm not sure about my mom, but I remember how flustered my dad became whenever he forgot to pick me up at school and how he then tried to make it up to me. Maybe Taylor's right, maybe Mom feels guilty all the time so it's become normal and I don't even notice it, and Dad only feels guilty when he makes glaringly obvious parental errors.

"As a matter of fact," says Taylor, "now I remember—that's how Erika got Bunga. Mom felt so guilty about putting her in daycare when she went back to work after Dad left that she bought her a puppy. And Erika had only been talking about wanting one for about five minutes."

"A horse is a lot bigger than a puppy," I say.

"You'd need a ton of guilt," Taylor advises.

CHAPTER EIGHTEEN

I'm riding Nickers, bareback of course, and we're out in a field doing canter figure-eights exactly like I saw Kansas do on Hambone. Nickers seems to know what she's doing or maybe I'm guiding her with my thoughts because we're doing perfect little circles and each time we get to the center of the eight I feel a small bump which must be her doing a flying lead change, and then we're cantering a circle in the other direction. We're not going flat-out, it's all very controlled and deliberate and it is so magically, wonderfully harmonious I don't think I've ever felt happier in my life.

I stay in the dream as long as I can. We canter across the meadow and then along a trail in the woods. I can hear birds singing and a rabbit runs down the path ahead of us. Everything's perfect until I start worrying that maybe that grumpy unicorn is going to pop out from behind a tree and will want to talk about whatever is wrong with me, and that's when I wake up.

I lie in bed for a while, because it's Saturday. I miss my barnacles. I miss having something to take care of other than me. But I'm not going to re-capture them.

Instead I decide to get up and make French toast for Mom and Dad to have in bed again, because I need some free time out on my bike. I'm not waiting until I'm cured by Dr. Gelderlander before seeing Kansas again.

The carbs and sugar from the syrup have the desired effect. I don't bring them any coffee. They start cuddling and yawning and I tell them I'm going to ride my bike to the mall and I'll be careful, but they are so far gone they hardly notice. None of what I tell them is a lie; I just omit saying anything about the side-trip I'm planning on the way home.

First I go to the Dollar Store to buy some horse stickers. When I'm there I'm surprised to find quite a lot of other stuff that will be excellent for my campaign. Some things would not normally be to my tastes—for example, the pink pens with white plastic pony heads stuck on the ends. But I also find some little black napkins with golden horseshoes on them, and a candle with a rearing palomino on one side that is drawn pretty much in proportion. Then I find something really funny that especially my Dad will like: a package of toilet paper covered with cartoon drawings of horse bums, just the back two legs and the tail, and the funniest part is that the tail is lifted exactly like a horse does before it starts to poop. Dad is going to kill himself laughing when he sees this. I buy two packs. In total I spend all but $5 of the cash that Auntie Sally gave me for Christmas.

My bike is locked in the rack outside the thrift store. I'm standing beside it trying to stuff all the things from the Dollar Store into my backpack without wrecking anything when something in the window display catches my attention. For a few seconds I can't believe my eyes because right there beside some pink and white snow boots is a small pair of chocolate-brown leather laced ankle boots. I step close to the window for a better look. I have to put my face right up against the glass with my hands like blinkers beside my eyes to block out my reflection, and only then am I sure. These are Ariats. I see the logo stamped in the leather at the ankle, exactly like I've seen in the equestrian supply catalogue. I know the model and all the details. These are the Junior Performer Paddock Boots. They hardly look used. They are worth about $100 new. I know all about these boots. They're made of water resistant leather. They have forged steel shanks, a patented lateral motion control device and a dual direction traction system to make them comfortable in the stirrup and yet stable while walking. They have self-cleaning treads so you don't track horse poop into the house. They have spur-rests on the heels. Spur rests. What can be better than that? But then I put my palm on the window to steady myself, because in fact there is something better: someone has stuck a strip of masking tape across one toe cap and what they've printed on it tells me not only that these boots are one size bigger than mine, making them ideal for growing into, but also that they want $4 for them.

When I come out of the thrift store, I have to take everything I bought at the Dollar Store out of my backpack, put the boots carefully in the bottom and then re-load, making sure that nothing is going to scratch the leather. This is the best, most exciting purchase I have ever made in my life.

I leap on my bike and fly off to see Kansas. I don't have much time before Mom and Dad's attention will drift back in my direction. I'm not planning on telling her about the boots. They can be a surprise one day when I show up for a lesson, perfectly attired. And it's just as well, because when I get there Kansas has company. There's a strange truck right beside the barn in the no-parking zone.

"Hey," says Kansas. I'm so happy to see her it that I'm afraid my face might split from smiling. She's holding Electra for a horseshoer who is bent over, pressing what must be a very hot shoe against the bottom of Electra's foot. There's smoke pouring out all over the place. Kansas is watching the horseshoer closely, which is understandable under the circumstances. I can hear sizzling and smell burning hoof, though Electra doesn't seem to mind.

Eventually, Kansas introduces us. "Sylvia, this is Declan, my new farrier," she says.

Declan doesn't say anything; maybe he nods his head when I say hi, but I'm not sure. He takes the shoe to his anvil, bangs it a couple of times with his hammer, throws it in a bucket of water for a few seconds, then fishes it out along with another shoe and brings them back to Electra. He loads some nails in his mouth with the sharp ends pointing out, like Auntie Sally holds the pins in her lips when she's doing her sewing. He picks up Electra's foot, holds her leg between his knees, and positions a shoe on the bottom of her hoof. He takes one nail out at a time, lines it up carefully, then hammers it through a hole in the shoe and into Electra's foot, with three quick blows. I can see the sharp end of the nail emerge through the hoof wall; he twists it off with the back end of his hammer, then repeats everything with the next nail.

Kansas is watching his every move. I don't blame her. I know from my reading that if a nail went in the wrong direction and ended up in the sensitive laminae inside the hoof wall, it would be very bad for the horse.

"Where've you been?" says Kansas. "I was afraid you'd moved." She doesn't sound very afraid. She sounds unfocussed and distracted. She doesn't take her eyes off Declan. He's wearing a t-shirt that, in my opinion, is on the small side for him, and he's sweating. He's more muscley than my dad.

"I'm kind of grounded," I say.

This seems to grab her attention, though not in the way I

would have expected. She turns to me and laughs. "Grounded? Parents are still doing that—punishing the whole family in one fell swoop?"

"Not officially." I've never thought of it this way before, that my parents were being punished by having to spend more time with me.

"Well, what did you do?" asks Kansas. "I had the impression you were a good kid."

"I am! They don't understand me, and they found some stuff on the computer that made it look like I'm . . . ." I stop because I don't know how to explain, and I expect someone to finish the sentence for me, but no one does, so I take my time and finally it comes to me. "They think I'm troubled."

Declan has finished with one shoe. He lowers Electra's foot and moves to her other side. She's holding up the new foot before he gets there.

"Are you?" says Kansas.

"I want a horse. That's all."

Declan takes all the nails out of his mouth and holds them between his thumb and finger. "That's trouble," he says, then spits, wipes his lips on his sleeve and puts the nails back in.

"That's good news for you, Declan," says Kansas with a warm laugh. "You've got another potential paying customer here." She's smiling at him. She looks all sparky. She's still dressed like one of the mannequins at the thrift store, and her hair is pulled back in a fat blue elastic, and she's wearing rubber boots, but she seems to have more energy than usual. Mostly when I see her around the horses she seems more on the mature, placid side. Today something about her reminds me of those kids from my school who my mom says need to be on Ritalin because there are limits, she is sorry to admit, to the benefits of non-biological interventions.

But I'm thinking something else is going on with Kansas. I'm thinking that quite possibly she is not a lesbian.

"We're putting shoes on Electra so you can start taking riding lessons. See—the ring is finished." She points with her free hand and I take in the riding ring beside the barn. It's like a great flat sandy beach surrounded by white board fencing. But the look of pride on Kansas' face tells me how important this is.

"Best outdoor arena in town," says Declan, hammering in the last nail.

"You think so?" says Kansas.

Declan doesn't answer. From anyone else this would be rude, but I have the impression he doesn't talk much. He lowers Electra's foot, straightens and examines his work. He grabs another tool, picks up a hoof and clenches down the ends of the nails that are poking through the outside of the hoof wall. He does the same thing with the other foot. "Just front shoes should be fine for now," he says. "See how she holds up. We can put backs on if she gets footy." He picks up his tool box and slides it into the back of his truck.

Kansas hands me Electra's lead rope and tells me to hang on to her for a minute. She returns from the tack room with a stack of pamphlets which she offers to Declan. "I had these printed up to advertise riding lessons and boarding. Maybe you could take them with you on your rounds?"

"It would be my pleasure." He reads the top one, then pulls it off and gives it to me. "For your parents," he says.

There's a photograph of Kansas on the back. She's wearing a white blouse with a high collar, a yellow vest and a black jacket with gold buttons. On her head is a man's top hat. It's the uniform of the upper-level dressage rider. I knew she was good, but this surprises me. I look over at her and she's watching Declan drive off. She doesn't look anything like the picture. "There goes the only Irishman I've ever met who couldn't talk the ears off a field of corn," she says.

Declan's truck turns the corner and disappears down the road and Kansas comes back to me and Electra.

"He wasn't wearing a wedding ring," I tell her.

She laughs. "What are you, fourteen or twenty-five?"

"I dunno. I just notice things."

"Well farriers never wear rings," she says. "Working all day with hot metal, hammers and lead ropes, they probably need to keep their fingers clear. When do you want to start your lessons?"

I hadn't planned on telling her, but it spills out of me. "I have to see a psychiatrist first."

"You're kidding me."

I shake my head.

"Sylvia, are you okay?" She sounds deeply concerned, but not panicked. Not frightened. Not anxious. It's a tremendous comfort to me, like being wrapped in a soft warm blanket.

"I think there's something wrong with me but I don't know what it is."

She nods her head as though she understands and doesn't need to argue with me or change my mind or make a point. "So how do you know?"

I shrug. Really, I don't know.

"Well maybe seeing a shrink is a good idea then."

"I guess."

"And after that you can start riding lessons. And after you've learned to ride you can start looking for a horse, maybe."

A horse. My own horse. My breathing quickens and my heart pounds in my ears and my brain gets so excited I can't think straight. I have to focus on something or I'm going to pitch over in a faint. I flip Kansas's pamphlet and read the list of services and prices on the back. Lessons, boarding, training, consultations.

"I can give you a special rate on the lessons if you can come around and help out."

I nod. I'm having to breathe through my mouth just to get enough air in my lungs, so even if I could think of something to say I probably couldn't get the words out. Not that there are any words coming to mind. Maybe I've been infected by Declan, who hardly says anything at all. I force myself to take a couple of controlled deep breaths. I look at my bike, leaning on the barn wall. My bike, which some day might be replaced by my horse, if only I can get my parents to agree. I check my watch. "I better go. They don't know I'm here."

"Thanks for coming, Sylvia. It was great to see you again. Let me know if I can help with the parents. Us horse people have to stick together."

I hold up the pamphlet. "This will help." Then I tuck it into my backpack behind the horse-butt toilet paper, and head on home.

She wasn't just being polite, I could tell from her voice. She really did like seeing me again. She likes me, and she doesn't have to, I'm not even family. Well, not biological family. I'm part of the herd.

I'm late getting home. Mom is on the driveway looking up the road for me. She's pretending not to, she's trying to make it look like she's doing something with the garbage cans, but she never does this because it's one of Dad's jobs and besides, the collector truck doesn't come until Monday. When I get off my bike she inspects the tires and somehow manages to identify horse poop stuck in the treads. I can't deny the possibility and I'm not going to lie. So the result is that she is very disappointed in me and at dinner time she and Dad use the United Front Technique (which I have never been able to

distinguish from piling on) and they make it very clear that
(1) I am going to take ballet lessons and (2) I am going to
see Dr. Gelderlander as soon as he can give me an appointment and (3) a horse is not in my near future.

CHAPTER NINETEEN

The unicorn is walking along grumpily, not talking to me. I can't understand what Taylor likes about these creatures. Maybe if she actually met one she'd see they aren't the perfect, kind, spiritual beings she thinks they are.

"My feet are sore," he says finally.

"Well maybe you should get shoes like . . . like the hornless ones get."

He rolls his eyes. "Oh please."

His horn is even shorter than last time, but I'm not about to mention it, not with him already being in a bad mood.

I notice I'm wearing my ballet outfit again. Then I think well, if it's my dream, at least I should be able to control what I'm wearing. And I think how I'd like to be dressed in a dressage outfit like Kansas was wearing for her photo on her pamphlet. So I look down again and the pink slippers have been replaced with tall black riding boots and spurs that jingle. "Ho-ly!"

"You're getting a little ahead of yourself," says the unicorn. "You still have to deal with the ballet lessons and whatever it is that's wrong with you."

"You mean you don't know what's wrong with me?"

"Not exactly. It's not my area. I report on the general picture."

"Do you mean the general spiritual picture?"

"I suppose," he says uncertainly. "But first could you define spiritual for me?"

This strikes me as ludicrous. "Look, you're the unicorn. If you don't know what spiritual means already then I'm sure not going to be able to describe it for you." And because I'm frustrated with everything I forget the rules and add, "You should be talking to my cousin Taylor if you want to know what spiritual means."

"Oh you've done it again," says the unicorn.

And just like that, there's Taylor walking beside me in the dream.

"Hey, good to see you," she says to me. "Nice outfit."

I check out my feet. I'm back in the ballet slippers.

She takes me by my shoulders and turns me so I'm facing her and she looks down and studies me carefully. "Though somehow a tutu doesn't really suit you."

That's when she sees the unicorn and screams.

"Oh lord," says the unicorn.

I take Taylor's hand. "It's only a unicorn."

"Thanks a lot," says the unicorn.

"You've got pictures of them all over your bedroom, and you saw one before, in my other dream."

Taylor is taking deep breaths. "Yes, but I've never seen a live one so close before." She grabs my arm and positions me between herself and the unicorn. "That horn looks deadly."

"You should see my teeth," says the unicorn; then he smiles at her.

"You know, for a herbivore, those are pretty pointy," I tell him.

I can feel Taylor quivering against me and then I hear her whimper.

"This isn't fair," I say, and wake myself up.

Mom and Dad have a quick round of couple's golf in the morning, which gives me time to plant my horse stickers around the place before Mom takes me to Auntie Sally's for lunch.

I put stickers in Mom's appointment book, tastefully, and not obscuring any important information like client names. I put my biggest sticker on the back of Dad's BlackBerry. I figure there's no sense being subtle any more. Now it's outright war, no guerillas.

I put the horse pens in Dad's briefcase, getting them all lined up in the loop holders so that the shiny blonde manes of the pony heads are fluffed out in a perfect row. The candle with the rearing palomino goes in the middle of the dining room table. The horseshoe napkins I arrange in a fan shape on the coffee table in the living room. I put more horse stickers around the computer monitor, and one on every light switch in the house. I steal a postage stamp from Mom's desk and stick it on a corner of Kansas's pamphlet, which I'm going to hide inside the mail when it comes tomorrow. I think this is a sly touch and much better than handing it to them. Let them think that the universe is in on my campaign and that resistance is futile.

When Mom and Dad come home it seems they have a campaign of their own, a new approach which could be titled "Don't React". I know they noticed. I saw Mom's fingers brush the sticker on the light switch beside the kitchen door, then she had a good long look at it, turned the light off and that was that. So before we leave for Auntie Sally's I put the horse-butt toilet paper in the dispenser in the main bathroom and in my parents' ensuite.

We're on the way to Auntie Sally's and stop at the intersection at the top of the hill on Lansdowne Street. I know this is a particularly long light so I take the opportunity to let Mom know that I won't be giving in to her other little plan. "No ballet," I say, but I've misjudged the light, which turns from red to green, and Mom must do something wrong with the car because it stalls.

"This stupid idiotic car!" says Mom.

"Taylor told me that you want her to talk me into it, and it's not going to happen."

"Really, Cookie, I can't . . . If this car doesn't start in two seconds I am going to scream."

"I understand, Mom, but I am not going to ballet lessons. I want riding lessons."

Then the ignition catches, the car lurches ahead and I think it's going to stall again but Mom floors it and we scoot on through the intersection just as the light turns from amber to red. Mom slaps the steering wheel with the palm of her hand. "Yes! Good old girl!" And she turns to me and smiles and says, "What was that, Peaches?"

I'm so mad I can't say anything. I'm sure she heard me. Probably she stalled the car on purpose. Obviously she will go to any ends to get what she wants. Well I've got news for her. So will I.

"No B-A-L-L-E-T."

"Careful, Cupcake. You're getting oppositional." She turns her head and fixes her sight on the road ahead of us.

"Mom, I'm not being oppositional. I'm standing up for myself, because I have high self-esteem."

In profile, my mom's face is somehow more readable. She can't paste on her professional psychoanalyst non-expression, and hide her true feelings. She licks her lips and swallows. "I see," she says.

And I think I should leave it at that for now.

When we arrive at Auntie Sally's lunch isn't ready because Auntie Sally and Taylor are studying home-decorating magazines. There's a stack of them on the kitchen table; Auntie Sally must have been collecting them for years.

"Isn't this exciting?" says Auntie Sally. "Finally Taylor wants a change in motif and we can be rid of those unicorns."

Taylor is looking more than a little tense and it's not just my imagination. She is flipping rapidly through a magazine with one hand and holding off Erika with another. I feel sick with responsibility.

"As long as you don't give me the hand-me-downs," says Erika. "I do not want Taylor's silly old unicorns in my bedroom. I want something new too." She slips past Taylor, grabs a magazine, opens it and immediately shoves the page at her mom. "I like this one. Look at all the Dalmatians! They're so cute." Then she stamps her foot and her eyes well up with tears, which seems premature to me—no one's said no yet. "It's not fair, Taylor gets everything."

I step in beside Taylor, who I figure is more in need of emotional support than decorating ideas. "What's up?" I whisper, but I'm afraid I already know the answer. "I thought you really liked unicorns."

She bites her lip. "I don't know. When I woke up this morning I looked around my room and all those unicorns totally creeped me out. They look unnatural and freaky, not spiritual at all. I can't explain it."

"Maybe you had a bad dream?" I prompt.

She shakes her head. "I don't dream."

"We all dream," corrects my mom. I should have known that talking quietly would only draw her attention.

"Mom, please," I say. "Taylor doesn't need a psychology lecture here."

Mom stiffens but carries on anyway. "Well I was merely going to say that if we don't get REM sleep, which is when we dream, then our brains don't function properly. Perhaps Taylor just doesn't remember her dreams." She opens a magazine and idly turns the pages, as though her feelings aren't hurt, but I know they are.

"I never dream," Taylor murmurs.

"Never?" I say. This is so sad. If I couldn't remember my dreams I'd lose at least half of what I enjoy about my life.

I hook my arm in hers. Fortunately she's not quivering the way she did in my dream, but the feel of her beside me is familiar and brings up a strong desire to protect her. This is all my fault and I don't have a clue how to fix it. I wish I did know; Taylor has tried hard to be helpful to me and in return I have ruined her life. Auntie Sally doesn't even seem to notice, she's so happy to have a decorating project in her sights. And Erika only thinks about Erika. Stephanie's away at university and probably wouldn't understand anyway. There's only one person who might be able to help, and so—with great reluctance, because I know how much she'll enjoy being consulted—I turn back to my mom. "What if she was scared by a dream but then she forgot the dream. How would she get over it? How would she learn to not be frightened of something if she didn't know why it scared her in the first place?"

"I don't know, Honey, though I suppose that's how anxiety disorders tend to manifest."

This is not what I was hoping for; I wasn't trying to get Taylor diagnosed with a mental illness, but I should have known that's what Mom would do with the situation. If I don't move fast, Mom will start scheduling therapy sessions. "She doesn't have an anxiety disorder! She had a bad dream about a stupid unicorn with sharp teeth and he scared her, that's all!"

They are all looking at me.

"Well, theoretically." I grab a magazine and flip through several pages. "Something floral would be nice for you, Taylor," I say, desperately looking for examples.

Unfortunately, disagreeing with Mom again has taken its toll. She says to Auntie Sally, "Sylvie's taken quite the sudden interest in interior decorating. You should see what she's doing at our house."

Auntie Sally completely misses the irony. "That's great," she says.

Mom takes another stab at getting control of the situation. "You know, Sally, I think that often a parent's job isn't so much to provide for every whim as it is to set limits, to say no, to let a child experience the reality that they are not always going to get what they want. Especially if what they want is expensive and beyond the family budget."

Auntie Sally flips a hand in Mom's direction. "Evelyn, you're sounding just like Tony."

Mom has a frustrated expression on her face that I don't see very often because any time she gets frustrated with me she turns it into a teaching opportunity, which is one of her life's great pleasures. "Sally, don't you remember what it was like when we were kids and Dad gave us anything we wanted? And Mom went around in those old dresses scrounging things she wanted out of garage sales? Didn't you feel guilty about that?"

Auntie Sally frowns. "I thought Mom liked getting stuff from garage sales. She never complained to me."

Mom shakes her head. "Well I'm not making the same mistake with my daughter." She reaches over and squeezes my shoulder.

I'm in a state of confusion sorting through this new information about Grandma and Grandpa and my mom's childhood. I wonder how guilty I would feel if Grandpa bought me a horse and Mom was still struggling along with her old car.

Auntie Sally gives my mom a penetrating look. "You know, Evelyn, you think too much. As a matter of fact you've always thought too much. I think you should loosen up a little." She returns her attention to the magazines on the table and puts an arm around Taylor. "Maybe it's time we all re-decorated. Maybe we could all use a change. We'll have to have a talk with Grandpa about this when he comes out for his visit."

"Grandpa's coming?" I stare at my mom. "No one told me."

CHAPTER TWENTY

On Wednesday Dad has an afternoon meeting so I'm allowed to ride my bike to school. I spend the whole day plotting how to see Kansas. In math class, Mr. Brumby yells at me to pay attention, which has never happened before, and it's really embarrassing even before Amber makes a crack about me being lost in outer space searching for my home planet.

Mom made me promise I wouldn't stop on my way home from school, and I don't want to lie but I'm desperate to see Kansas. I need time with my herd—even a minute would help. My plan is to ride my bike to Kansas's gate, hop off, open the gate, roll my bike through, close the gate, pedal up her driveway and then ride circles in front of the barn while I talk to her before riding home. No stopping, that's what Mom said, and if I'm in constant motion, then technically I won't be disobeying her.

I'm on my bike ready to leave the school grounds when Mom's car lurches into the parking lot. Mom leaves the engine running (loosely speaking), and opens the trunk. "Dr.

Gelderlander's office called. They have a cancellation if we can get there by 3:30."

While Mom wrestles with my bike I climb in the front seat. I stare at the ignition key, wondering which way I would have to turn it to shut off the engine, and whether Mom would notice what I'd done. I decide it's not worth the risk, and with my luck this would be the one time in recorded history that the car re-started.

Amber and Topaz and Logan Losino walk by. Amber holds her nose and flaps at the exhaust fumes coming out of the car. Topaz says, "Apparently some people still don't believe in global warming."

But when they've passed us, Logan turns around and I'm not positive, but I think he rolls his eyes.

"He's cute," says Mom, sliding into her seat.

"Who?"

"That boy." She points at Logan's departing back.

"Mom, don't point!"

"Don't you think he's cute?"

"You're being gross."

"No need to be rude, Sylvie."

I fold my arms and slouch into the seat so I'm well out of sight when we pass the kids on the road. Mom gives them a finger-wave anyway. I could die.

"Honey, what we need to decide before we get to Dr. Gelderlander's office is whether or not I should come in with you."

I try to imagine which would be worse: listening to my mom fully describe my problems in psychoanalytic lingo, or being alone with a strange doctor and having to tell him the personal facts of my life.

"Is he going to be like John?"

"Well sort of, Sweetie, but not really. John is a psychologist

but Dr. Gelderlander is a medical doctor who has special-
ized in psychiatry."

This is bad news and brings up my other fear. "He's not
going to examine me is he?"

"Well no, Cupcake, not physically. Or at least I don't
think so." She doesn't sound sure. I'm not liking this.

"Maybe you should come in with me," I say.

"Well, of course I can, at least to begin with. I can help get
things started, and put things in perspective," she says in an
enthusiastic way which leaves me regretting my suggestion.

Dr. Gelderlander's office is at the hospital. It takes us ten
minutes of circling in the parking lot to find a space that
Mom thinks she can squeeze the car into. Then we go in
the wrong door and obviously Mom doesn't know where
we're supposed to be so eventually we go back to the main
lobby and find the information desk and by the time Mom
pulls me by the hand down this really long hallway and we're
standing in front of a door marked "Child and Adolescent
Psychiatric Programs", she's breathing hard and it's 3:35.

I'm hoping we're too late and they've given my appointment to someone else. If not, I'm hoping that if we go in
right away Mom will be too out of breath to talk or better
yet that she'll be so tired she'll decide to sit in the waiting
room and rest.

Mom pats her hair into place, opens the door and then
kind of hip-checks me until I'm walking ahead of her over
to the reception desk.

"Sorry we're late," Mom says over my head. I can hear her
panting but it isn't preventing her from talking. She puts her
hands on my shoulders. "This is Sylvie, to see Dr. Gelderlander for 3:30."

The receptionist looks up from her computer screen and
smiles. "No problem, we're running a little late here anyway." She hands Mom a form to fill out on a clipboard,

which is very discouraging because this is going to give her time to rest up. Then there's more bad news because the receptionist says, "But they did tell you that Dr. Gelderlander isn't actually here today and that Sylvie will be seeing his locum, Dr. Cleveland?"

"Who," says Mom, having so carefully researched the most suitable therapist for me, "is Dr. Cleveland?" I can hear the icicles in her voice. Obviously she's not too tired to turn into indignant super-mom.

I slink away to a chair against the far wall. I don't want to participate in the interrogation and I'd rather not listen to it either. I plant my elbows on my knees and cover my ears with my hands. It doesn't work, I can still hear them.

"Oh she's great, everyone really likes her, we're so lucky to get her on such short notice," says the receptionist. She's still all chirpy. You'd think that anyone working with mentally ill people every day would be more aware when an atomic blast was about to go off.

Mom says, "What kind of experience does she have? Or is she fresh out of medical school?"

There's a slight pause. I guess the receptionist is trying to decide if that was really irony she heard. "Well I'm not sure about that, but she's really nice."

"How wonderful. Unfortunately, I'm not looking for nice. I was thinking more along the lines of astute, competent and experienced."

I don't know when I've heard my mom sound this angry. Even Dad says that when Mom doesn't have her way she becomes either sarcastic or scholastic. But I do know how relentless she can be, so to save myself further embarrassment I say, "Mom, please—I'll be fine."

She looks over at me, then back at the receptionist, whose smile has disappeared. Then she comes back and sits beside me. She takes a pen out of her purse and sets to work on the form but I can tell she's still fuming. "This is ridiculous," she mutters. "They should already have all this information. We had a referral from Dr. Destrie, you'd think his office would have provided the pertinent medical history."

"It's probably in the mail. We got a cancellation, remember?"

"They could have faxed it. Or sent it by computer."

"You think Dr. Destrie has heard of computers?"

Mom turns the page over and sighs again.

I put my head in my hands and stare at the floor. I feel like throwing up. Partly it's the smell of the hospital, which I remember from when I visited Grandma before she died and Uncle Brian when he was sick, but mostly it's because the medical atmosphere has convinced me that I am going to be subjected to a physical examination, and if there is any question of sexual orientation, hermaphrodism or bisexuality I am sure I know where they're going to be looking. The fact that my mother will be in the room with me only makes it worse.

I hear the door to the hallway open and close but I don't look up. The receptionist says, "Oh hi, Dr. Cleveland, your 3:30 is here."

Dr. Cleveland's legs and feet cross my line of vision— black pants and some kind of flat-soled black shoes. I'm surprised because I guess I was expecting nylons and heels, like Mom wears to work because she says it's important to always look professional.

Mom gets to her feet, then tugs on my sleeve. "Come on, Lambchop. Off to the lion's den."

This must be a joke for Dr. Cleveland's benefit because it sure doesn't tickle my funny bone. I stand up as slowly as I can.

I expect Dr. Cleveland to be old, like Mom, but she's not. She's tall and slender and curvy and beautiful. She's everything I'm not and never will be. She takes the clipboard from Mom. "Usually I start my interview without the parents." She runs a finger back and forth across the page, reading. "But I suppose, as a professional courtesy . . . "

Great. Mom has managed to record her profession on my form. My life is over. This is going to be terrible. Two against one.

CHAPTER TWENTY-ONE

There's a desk at the far end of the room under the window, but closer to the door is a small sitting area with five uphol-stered chairs and a side-table. In the middle of the table is a box of tissues and beside it there's a file folder with my name on the tab.

My mom takes a chair and motions for me to sit beside her. In an open act of rebellion I take a chair across from her and sit in it, arms folded. She and Dr. Cleveland can talk all they want—I'm staying out of it.

Dr. Cleveland sits beside Mom. Dr. Cleveland's posture is perfect. She's like a perfect composed picture of what a woman should be. Her hair is black and shiny. Her skin is flawless creamy-brown. There is a faint spray of freckles across her little nose. She flips open the file folder and reads out loud from Dr. Destrie's note, handwritten on a page from his prescription pad. "Please see Syl re: difficulties." She clears her throat. "Not the most in-depth referral I've ever received. Do you go by Syl? Sylvia? Or . . . ?"

I have the feeling she's about to add Lambchop to the

list, and maybe Mom does too because she bursts in saying, "Sylvie."

Dr. Cleveland doesn't take her eyes off me. She ignores Mom, who is opening her mouth, maybe to repeat herself, maybe thinking she wasn't heard the first time, so I say, "Sylvia," perhaps too emphatically because Dr. Cleveland jumps a little.

She picks up the clipboard and checks the form again. "So you're fourteen?"

"Going on fifteen," I say, which is a stretch, but I'm daring her to say something about my size.

She nods and smiles. "Of course. And how's life so far?"

"It's okay."

"And you're here because . . . ?"

I point a thumb towards Mom.

"Your mom," she says, and I nod. She turns the form over and peers at my mom's handwriting, then holds the form out to her with her finger under one word. "What's this one say?"

Mom takes a quick peak. "Puberty," she says.

Dr. Cleveland takes the form back and reads some more. I feel sorry for her. My mom's handwriting is really terrible. I lean back in my chair—this could take a while. I look at the certificates on the wall, all with Dr. Gelderlander's name on them. I survey the bookcase, the desk, the carpet. My mom is wearing her good beige pumps that coordinate with her beige skirt and jacket. Dr. Cleveland is wearing . . . I look away, and look back again to be sure. I can't believe it. I stare at her feet. There is the plain toecap, the reinforced outer sole at the instep. She crosses her legs in front of her and I lean sideways, hanging on to the arm of the chair, until I spy the spur rests. She's wearing Ariat paddock boots. I search her face. Could she be a member of the herd? It is too much to hope for, but still the thought overwhelms me and I say, "There's some question about my sexual orientation."

She looks up and studies me carefully, nodding slowly all the time. "Do you have much sexual experience?" She doesn't look over at Mom once, not even with the slightest glance. Her attention is focused completely on me.

"No." I stare at her, watching for a sign. The rest of the room disappears.

"I see. Well then, maybe you could tell me, even though you don't have actual experience, what about fantasies? Do you dream about kissing boys or girls?"

I only know of one dream which involved a kiss. I feel like my life is hanging by a thread. If Dr. Cleveland is a horse-woman, she'll understand and maybe she'll be able to save me, though if she lets on that she's a member of the herd I know she'll lose all credibility with my mom. "I dreamt I kissed a horse once."

A little groan comes from Mom's direction but Dr. Cleveland ignores her. Her eyebrows have gone up as though she's on to something. "You like horses?"

I can't speak—any answer I can think of would only be an understatement, like trying to answer a question about how much I liked breathing. I manage one short sharp nod then I stare pointedly at her boots and say, "My mom doesn't."

Mom mistakes this as a cue and clears her throat. I imagine with dread her launching into her notion of horseback riding as an early adolescent phallic activity.

I'm watching Dr. Cleveland. She looks from me to her boots. Then she looks to my mom and back to me again. "I understand," she says and I see that there is more to her than physical perfection, more even than being a member of the herd. She is some kind of boss mare.

I tell her everything. I tell her about Grandpa, and about dreaming of horses, though I leave out the unicorn. I tell her about my friend Kansas, who makes up for not having friends at school. I tell her about not wanting to do ballet. I tell her about the barnacle project and how they are hermaphrodites (she didn't know) and how doing the research on the computer started the whole bisexuality question. I talk longer than I've ever talked in my life. I talk so much my tongue aches.

And when I'm finished she nods some more and looks out the window for a while and then she asks me some questions about how well I sleep and how well I eat and what kind of grades I'm getting at school and then she says, "Well, Sylvia, I'd have to say that from a psychiatric point of view there doesn't seem to be much of a problem here."

I see Mom check her watch and pull her purse into her lap. I can't read her expression which has gone blank again. But I'm nowhere near ready to leave yet, because there's another matter to deal with.

"But there's still something wrong with me," I insist because I know she knows and that finally, finally we are going to get to the bottom of it.

"Yes, I think so." Dr. Cleveland laces her fingers in her lap and considers them for a moment before saying, "I'm concerned about what's happening for you socially at school because kids are pretty observant. I think they've noticed how unusual you are. Physically, I mean."

"Like how short I am."

"Right. You should be taller. You're pretty well off the bottom of the growth charts."

"We've been expecting a growth spurt any day now," says Mom.

"Of course," says Dr. Cleveland, kindly I think.

"I do stretches—all the time. And I try to eat lots of protein. And I don't smoke."

"Well that's all good, but I don't think it's going to be

enough. I think there's a chromosomal problem, something you were born with. Ideally this could have been addressed sooner, but we might still be able to do something about it. We're a bit late, but possibly not too late."

Mom shifts in her chair. Her eyes are big. Dr. Cleveland says to her, "It's not uncommon for family doctors to miss some things, especially in children who are otherwise high-functioning. And not a lot of parents catch the signs."

Not a lot, I think, but some. Mom won't be happy about this.

Dr. Cleveland asks for my hand and looks at my palm, like Taylor did when she was trying to read my future, only Dr. Cleveland doesn't sound surprised at what she finds. She traces the single horizontal line on my palm with her finger. "Sometimes this is called a simian crease," she says. Then she asks me to make a fist. She shows me her fist for comparison. She has four bumpy knuckles and I only have three. "You've got abnormal bone development, which is another indicator."

My Mom cranes over to see, then checks her own fist. Her cheeks are pink.

"I've got a mane too," I say excitedly, flipping up my hair and turning so they both have a good view of the back of my neck. "Mom's hairdresser noticed, right, Mom? Is this part of it?"

"Smart girl," says Dr. Cleveland. "I think so."

"And my nails. They're kind of like claws." I hold my fingers out for inspection but she doesn't need to see.

"I already noticed. I wasn't going to mention them, in case you were self-conscious."

I stand up and step in front of her. I am at her eye level even though she is still seated in her chair. I feel like throwing my arms around her neck. "Are you kidding? This is the best day of my life."

165

"To be able to talk about these things?"

"Yes."

"If I'm right, there's treatment for some of what you're dealing with, but not all of it. Not the hairline, the nails."

"All I care about is my height. I have to get to five feet if Grandpa is going to buy me a horse."

"Pumpkin . . . ," says Mom. Her whole face is pink now.

"I'm going to be honest with you," says Dr. Cleveland. "I don't know if we can get you there."

"But you can try."

Mom's eyes are overflowing. I put a hand on her shoulder. "Mom, they can fix me. You don't have to be sad."

"Well Sylvia, I don't know about fixing you, but we can certainly treat some of your symptoms," says Dr. Cleveland. "Though not me, actually. I think you should see a pediatrician for a start. We need to confirm a diagnosis and check out a few other things."

"But I want to see you."

She thinks about this. "Maybe as a follow-up. I'll have to see if I there's a diagnostic code on my billing form for horse nut."

Mom doesn't get the joke. Her face is red and her eyes are streaming. I don't understand why she isn't relieved like I am that I'm not bisexual and that whatever is wrong with me is at least somewhat fixable, but she's looking so sad and frightened that I sit down beside her.

"A pediatrician?" she says. "What for, exactly?" She takes my hand and squeezes it so hard it hurts.

And then Dr. Cleveland tells us that she thinks I may have Turner Syndrome. I don't absorb much of what she says; I figure we can always go home and Google it to get the details. The one part that strikes me is when she talks about medication for my height. "There's a window of opportunity for treatment, usually prior to adolescence. With Sylvia being fourteen, we won't know if the window is still open for her, until she has some tests. If her epiphyses haven't closed, that is, if the growth plates at the ends of her long bones aren't fused yet, then she can be prescribed some growth-stimulating medication. It would be good for her to reach five feet."

This is truly amazing. For once it may be a good thing that I am a slow developer: my growth plates could still be open. I turn to Mom to see if she also understands the significance. She grabs a tissue, blows her nose then looks at us both suspiciously. "Five feet," she repeats.

"Generally speaking it helps people psychologically if they can break the five-foot barrier," explains Dr. Cleveland.

"Even people who aren't . . . ." My mom hesitates like a person attempting to say something in a totally foreign language, then takes another run at it. "Even people who aren't horse nuts?"

"Right," says Dr. Cleveland. She sits back in her chair, more relaxed now, as though the hard part is over. This makes me relax too. I pat the back of Mom's hand, which is white as chalk from gripping the arm of her chair.

"You should know," says Dr. Cleveland, "that in my experience being a horse nut is not a treatable condition."

Mom presses her lips so tight they almost disappear from her face.

"It's a wonderful thing, actually." Dr. Cleveland continues calmly as though she is completely unable to read parental facial expressions. She must have trained for years and years to learn to do this. "Some people never develop passions, they spend their lives wandering along aimlessly looking for something meaningful and fulfilling to do. I'm sure you've run into people like this in your practice."

Mom nods reluctantly. "Of course."

"Whereas some fortunate people discover very early in

their lives what is meaningful to them. And the luckiest of them find ways of pursuing their passion."

Mom doesn't say anything.

"I'm not saying you have to go out and buy a horse. Something like riding lessons would be a good start."

I hold my breath, hoping I don't turn blue.

"We were thinking ballet would be better exercise," says Mom. Now that we're not talking about my possibly having Turner Syndrome she's not upset any more. She's sounding more like her normal opinionated self.

"People who don't ride often find it difficult to believe how much physical fitness is required. Riding is great exercise when it's done properly, with a good instructor. There's nothing wrong with ballet, except that she doesn't want to do it."

"Oh," says Mom noncommittally.

I'm thinking Mom doesn't like being lectured to any more than I do. I'm hoping Dr. Cleveland leaves it at this and doesn't try to make any more of a point. Especially, I don't want her to talk about her own interest in horses, which is totally obvious to me, though Mom still doesn't get it. So I smile at Dr. Cleveland and say, "Thank you."

Dr. Cleveland smiles back and tucks her feet under her chair.

Mom says, "Well perhaps we can look into riding lessons after we've seen the pediatrician."

I take this as a huge breakthrough—it's all I can do to stay in my chair and not leap up screaming.

Mom snatches her appointment book out of her purse. "Are you absolutely sure we need another specialist? Dr. Destrie seems to think he can manage most things."

"I'm sure he does," says Dr. Cleveland. "How about I make the referral myself. No need to bother Dr. Destrie."

She tells Mom the name of the pediatrician and Mom

writes it in her book. She has to write overtop of one of my horse stickers, but doesn't say anything to me about this. Then they make an appointment for me to come back to see Dr. Cleveland in two months. There's a horse sticker on that page too, almost as if I'd known in advance, or it was destiny, or some spiritual thing.

Mom makes Mexican lasagna for dinner, which is my absolute favourite and she doesn't make it very often because she says it's too fussy. Dad has a late client and doesn't get home until Mom and I are at the table and Mom is carving the lasagna into squares. Before he can tell us about his day, I remind him about my appointment.

"Oh, right," he says. "So, how did it go?"

"She was really nice," I say. "And also very professional."

"She? I thought Gelderlander was a guy."

"We saw his locum, a rather young woman," says Mom. "Though I wonder if we should request another referral to see Dr. Gelderlander—for a second opinion." Mom lifts a serving of lasagna onto a plate and passes it to me.

"I don't want a second opinion," I tell her. Turning to Dad I say, "She says I'm a horse nut."

"That was her official diagnosis? Can she treat horse nuts?"

"I don't want treatment for that."

"She also thinks Sylvia may have something called Turner Syndrome," says Mom, passing a plate to Dad. "She wants her to see a pediatrician. She thinks that's why she's so short."

"She's a kid. All kids are short."

"Not this short," I say, grabbing the salad bowl.

"You mean there's really something wrong with her?" Dad asks Mom.

"And we missed it," says Mom.

I'm fishing around in the salad bowl for a couple more cherry tomatoes and suddenly it's as though all the tension and uncertainty and confusion I didn't even know I had flows out of me through the top of my head. I totally relax. It doesn't matter if I find another tomato, it doesn't matter if I spill a few lettuce leaves off the edge of my plate. For one glorious moment, everything is perfect and I am galloping unimpeded towards a future which stands open-armed and beckoning before me. This must be what Taylor means about being spiritual because I feel like my life is totally taken care of and everything will be okay, all I have to do is to let things unfold. No divorce, and no one has to move to a new neighbourhood. But the scent of guilt in the air is unmistakable. Along with it comes a sense of power I have never experienced before in my life, though it's not unlike the time that Logan Losino offered to beat someone up for me and I said sure and he said who and I picked some funny-looking boy from grade four and Logan said Who—Tony? And before I could stop him, before I could say oh no that's my dad's name, Logan had dumped Tony in the dirt and I felt sick.

I look up from the depths of the salad bowl.

Mom is cutting a piece of lasagna for herself. She always serves herself last. She is pressing so hard with the metal slicer that she's going to gouge the Corningware, which she's always telling me not to do. I think about reminding her, but then I see her face is going all pink again and I don't think it's from exertion or heat from the kitchen. She's trying not to cry. So I look at Dad. His fork is halfway to his mouth and he has a very stern look on his face, like he's angry with someone, but I can't think who that would be. I thought he would be happy that we didn't have to go to family therapy, but he doesn't look happy at all.

CHAPTER TWENTY-TWO

I wake up to my alarm and I haven't had a dream. I really could have used one because I have this feeling that everything is about to change and maybe things weren't really so bad before and maybe desperately wanting something isn't such a great idea.

Mom is reading Kansas's pamphlet at the breakfast table but she puts it down when I come in the room. "Look what we got in the mail," she says. She doesn't even try to sound surprised. The skin under her eyes is dark and saggy in a way I haven't seen before. I guess she didn't sleep well after our time spent doing research on the computer last night. When we finished dinner we Googled Turner Syndrome, which maybe wasn't the smartest thing to do because it turns out that some people with this disorder can get serious heart and kidney problems and I said I was positive that didn't apply to me and Mom said surely Dr. Destrie would have picked that up. Dad said only if there'd been big flashing signs pointing towards it and then he asked Mom if her university training was half as good as she said it was then why didn't she know about what was wrong with me. That's when I went to my room, did some stretches and crawled into bed. And thought about the other thing I saw about people with Turner Syndrome, that sometimes they have abnormal Y chromosome material. Sometimes they have testicular tissue that has to be removed by surgery. So I could be a kind of hermaphrodite after all, or a crypt orchid, just like Hambone.

I'm trying not to think about this possibility when I take my seat at the breakfast table. I perch lightly on the edge of my chair because the last thing I want is to notice whatever testicles might feel like if they were hidden up inside me.

Mom slides Kansas's brochure over to the edge of my placemat. I can see it's covered with Dad's handwriting, mostly numbers and dollar signs, so he's obviously done some calculations already.

My plan had been to act surprised and excited when the pamphlet appeared, but now I can't.

"She seems to be well-qualified, your friend Kansas," says Mom.

Dad is standing over the toaster trying to dislodge something that is thick and smoking. He wiggles the lever, presses it upwards and it snaps off in his hand. "Stupid effing toaster," he says under his breath, but not so quietly that I can't hear him. I guess he didn't sleep well either.

"Dad, it was a hundred years old, you got it as a wedding present."

He unplugs the toaster, turns it upside-down over the sink and sticks a table knife up into the slot. He looks like he's trying to stab it to death.

Mom sighs. I know she'd wanted a toaster for Christmas and Dad bought her winter tires instead. They had a big argument on Boxing Day because Mom said it didn't make sense to throw more money into that piece of junk and Dad said it had thousands of miles left in it and Mom said she wanted the tires returned and Dad said he couldn't return them because they weren't actually new, they were re-treads. He found them in the *Buy and Sell*.

"We think we can afford a trial series of riding lessons," Mom says to me.

Half a bagel lands heavily in the sink. Dad scrapes off the burnt bits with the knife and brings it to the table. He loads on the cream cheese so thick that I'm sure Mom's going to say something about his cholesterol levels but she just passes him the strawberry jam.

"So what do you say, Shor . . . " and he looks at Mom, then looks back at me, and says, "Sylvia."

I have never been more confused in my life. I should be so happy. Finally they aren't calling me stupid nicknames. Finally they are agreeing that I can take riding lessons. But they are both so unhappy, and I hate it when they're unhappy. I thought victory was supposed to be sweet. And I think, what is the point of being passionate about something if it only makes other people miserable? But I can't say this, I know this would only make things worse, so I say the only thing possible. "Thank you."

I ride my bike to school, where everything is normal, which is not to say good but at least I'm used to it. This will probably change too because Mom and Dad want a meeting with the principal, Mrs. Tarpan, to discuss my medical condition once it's confirmed by the pediatrician, and to remind her of the school's zero tolerance policy on bullying even though I tell them that I'm not really being bullied, it's more that I'm being picked on, which is really quite normal for kids, it's kind of like herd dynamics for horses. They tell me it's not a matter open for negotiation.

After school I stop in to see Kansas and she's nowhere around. I feel like I'm being left to sort this out completely on my own. I don't want to go home. I leave my bike leaning against the side of the barn and go looking for Hambone. I don't want to ride him now, not after seeing what he did when Kansas rode him, and besides I've promised not to. But I do want to hang out with him. He's not out in the pasture with the mares. I find him in his stall. There's a bandage around his right front leg from his knee to his fetlock, and there's a swelling about the shape of Electra's hind foot on his shoulder. I guess she had enough of his tactics and decided to show him who was really the boss.

I take the carrot sticks I've saved out of my backpack, open his stall door and slide in with him. He drops his head and nuzzles my hand. I feed him these tiny carrot sticks one at a time and he takes each one carefully with the edges of his lips. He never uses his teeth. I reach up and put my arms around his neck and tell him that everything's working out for me but it doesn't feel very good. I put my cheek against his neck and he is warm and smells good and I tell him I'm going to start lessons—not on him right away, but maybe one day. And I have the sense that even though I'm feeling rotten about getting my way and even though I don't know if I'll be brave enough or good enough to ride like Kansas, that if I have the opportunity this is still what I want to do more than anything else. I want to be with horses. I can't imagine my life without them. It's that simple and it's that complicated all at once.

It will be nice to be older one day and understand life better. It will be good to know with certainty what's right and what's wrong, but in the meantime I guess I can muddle through.

That night Mom phones Kansas and finds out what needs to happen before I start my lessons. I'm all excited because the most important thing is that I get my own helmet, which will be my very first piece of new riding equipment. Also

Mom and Dad have to sign a release form, which Dad isn't that happy about so he calls her back. When he gets off the phone his eyes are big. He clears his throat, then says to my mom, "Kansas tells me that waivers are standard industry practice and they are required by her insurance agency. So I suppose that will be fine."

Dad has run into the boss mare.

Then he turns to me. "Kansas tells me that under no circumstances am I to buy you a used helmet off eBay. We have to purchase a new one because that's the only way to be sure there aren't any hair-line fractures. I have the impression that she thinks I'm cheap. Where would she have gotten an idea like that?"

I can tell he's not kidding, and that he's more perplexed than angry. Can he really be the last one to know? "Well, Dad, you are very careful with your money," I say, trying to be gentle. Mom's looking wary. She finds the box of baking soda again and sets to work in the sink.

"Of course I'm careful with money," says Dad.

"And you always encourage us to buy used and to keep things going as long as possible . . . like Mom's car."

Mom pauses in her scouring, then runs some water down the drain.

"There's nothing wrong with your mom's car."

Mom straightens and stares at Dad. She's standing behind him, though, so he can't see the look of disbelief on her face. I hope she won't say anything, because things have been going pretty well between the two of them this evening and the last thing I want is a fresh dust-up. Besides, maybe this is something that would be better undertaken by me on Mom's behalf. "Dad, everything is wrong with Mom's car."

"Oh come on," says Dad. "Not everything. Besides, we'll replace it as soon as Mom's client list fills up and she pays off her student loan."

Mom shakes her head sadly but stops abruptly when Dad swivels around to bring her into the conversation. "Right, Evie?" he says.

She smiles stiffly. "Right."

I don't understand. There must be more going on here than I can grasp, kind of like herd dynamics again. It feels so complex I wouldn't even know what to Google to figure it out. And it reminds me of another matter that I don't understand. "Dad, why do you think Grandpa is an interfering old goat just because he says he'll buy me a horse some day?"

Dad frowns. For a second I'm not sure if he's going to be angry with me, but then he says, "Look, Shorty, adult relationships are complicated, there's a lot of history here. It has nothing to do with you."

I think it has everything to do with me, but Mom walks over and puts her hand on the back of Dad's neck. Her fingers slide through the curls above his collar.

"I shouldn't have said that about Grandpa," he says. "Or at least not where you could hear."

And even though this isn't much of an answer and I still don't understand, I have the feeling that I've pushed the matter as far as I can.

A few days later I get to see the pediatrician, Dr. Moyle. He's nice, but not as nice as Dr. Cleveland. He agrees tentatively with her diagnosis but won't say for sure until he sees the results of the blood work. We all go back a week later and he confirms that yes, it seems that I do have Turner Syndrome. I have to ask him explicitly if they found any Y chromosome material and he looks a bit flustered, but then he says no, so I am not a hermaphrodite, which is slightly disappointing because I would have liked to have something special in common with Hambone. But mostly it's a relief.

Because Dr. Moyle says he wants me to have more tests,

Mom and Dad get all uptight again and won't let me start my lessons with Kansas. They need to know that my heart and kidneys are okay though apparently it's fine for me to continue to ride my bike to school and take stupid phys ed class. Along with the tests I have referrals to see other medical specialists to check my eyes and my hearing and it looks like this is going to take years. But after a week I'm so unhappy sitting around at home doing nothing that we go back to Dr. Moyle for another discussion and some preliminary results, and he tells my parents that other than having Turner Syndrome I'm as healthy as a horse—no kidding, that's exactly what he says. And then he says something even more wonderful. He says that as well as taking supplements to help my bone strength I need to get lots of exercise. And I ask him if it has to be ballet and he says absolutely not.

CHAPTER TWENTY-THREE

The unicorn is limping beside me. He throws his weight off his right front foot any time it hits the ground.

"Can't you get that fixed?" I ask.

"As you know, not everything is fixable."

We walk some more. I look at his horn out of the corner of my eye. I'm pretty sure it's even shorter than last time but I'm not about to say anything.

"What?" he says.

I don't want to ask. He already seems more unhappy than usual. I decide on a diversion. Something else has been on my mind anyway. "My parents aren't very happy. I think it's my fault."

"It's not your fault. They just feel guilty—it's an essential ingredient of parenting."

"It's because of me."

"It's not your responsibility. It has nothing to do with you."

"Really?"

He grunts.

"That's what Dad said about his problem with Grandpa,

that it had nothing to do with me, but it seems to me it has everything to do with me. I don't understand why Dad isn't happy about Grandpa buying me a horse. I know Dad's really careful with his money, so why should he be upset if Grandpa wants to buy me something?"

"Your dad works very hard."

"I know that."

"And he pays for a lot of things that aren't very exciting. Like the mortgage. Like the dentist. Then Grandpa comes along and buys the fun stuff, and everyone loves him for it."

"I hadn't thought of it that way. I guess it makes sense. But why didn't he tell me?"

"He doesn't know."

I'm pondering this when the unicorn says, "So they think you have Turner Syndrome, do they?"

"They say I have only one X chromosome instead of two, like women are supposed to have."

"So you're not bisexual. You're semi-sexual." He snorts loudly at his own joke.

"Well at least they can fix some of it—they can help me grow taller. But I probably won't be able to have children."

"Oh well." He sounds sad, which surprises me.

"Who wants children? Especially if children make you feel guilty all the time. I want a horse."

He snorts again. "As if a hornless one will solve all your problems."

I tell him, "You're just grumpy because your foot is sore."

"You're just happy because your heart and kidneys are normal."

"Some people with Turner Syndrome aren't as lucky as me."

"So all of a sudden you think you're lucky?"

"Yeah. I do."

And I wake up, and I'm still feeling lucky, which is pretty strange. After all, I have a medical problem that went undiagnosed too long so I may always be short and I'll always look unusual and my ovaries will probably shrivel up. But my heart is fine and my kidneys are fine and my bones are strong and I don't have two competing sets of sexual organs which could make me accidentally pregnant if I jumped around too much. Things could be much worse.

But the main reason I'm feeling lucky is that today is my first riding lesson.

Dad insists on driving me. He says he wants to be sure everything's on the up and up. Mostly I think he wants to be sure to get a receipt for the cheque he's writing for the weekly lesson package. He has said something about writing it off as a medical expense.

Mom says she has some errands to do and she'll come later, which is strange, but since the first half of the first lesson is going to be about grooming and tacking up she doesn't need to be there anyway.

Dad stays in the car when we get there. Of course he has some calls to make.

I'm so excited I think I might throw up.

Kansas inspects me. She checks the fit of my helmet and adjusts the straps so it sits level on my head. Then she sees my feet. "Nice boots," she says.

Electra is already in the cross-ties in the alleyway in the barn. She doesn't look like she needs brushing, but I do it anyway. Kansas shows me the right brushes to use and I already know their names because of studying the Pony Club manual, but I've never actually had my hands on all of them before. Then she gives me a hoof pick and shows me how to ask Electra to pick up her feet so I can clean out the dirt, of which there isn't any. And I know that Kansas is so proud of Electra she's got her looking perfect for me, and she's proud

180

of me too, and she's pleased with herself that her business is starting and I'm just about vibrating with pleasure and nervous anticipation and that's when she stops.

"Sylvia, the most important thing is to be focused on your horse. I know you're excited, but you have to put that aside and think about Electra and how she's doing."

We stand back and look at her. Electra examines us calmly in response.

"She's standing square on all four feet," says Kansas. "She's not keeping her weight off anything that might be sore. Her ears are perked, she's paying attention, she looks bright and healthy and happy."

"Like me," I say.

Kansas reaches down and puts her arm around my shoulders and gives me a squeeze. "Let's tack her up."

And she shows me how to put on the bridle and the saddle. I know the names of all the parts, but getting everything on straight is another matter. I have to stand on a stool to make sure the saddle is centered on Electra's back, and it's hard work for my fingers to get the girth as tight as Kansas wants it, but I do it, and then I lead Electra out to the riding ring.

Kansas tells me to use the mounting block and points me to a set of wooden stairs going nowhere that are just inside the entry gate.

I don't want to be treated special just because I'm short so I say, "I don't need to use a mounting block. I can get on from the ground."

"Everyone uses a mounting block," says Kansas. "I use one. It's a kindness to the horse. You don't want to be pulling on her spine every time you haul yourself up into the saddle. You can learn to get on from the ground later—you'll need to know how for trail riding. But when you're in the ring, I want you to use the mounting block."

"Sorry," I say.

"It's okay, I understand."

Using the mounting block is kind of like getting on from the fence, like I used to do with Hambone, only easier. And I've never ridden in a saddle before. Kansas adjusts the stirrups to the right length, then attaches a lunge line to Electra's bridle and leads us to the middle of the arena. I feel Electra move underneath me. I'm not sliding around like I did bareback, but still, it's not steady, like riding a bike. I am way off the ground and completely out of control. It's not anything like my dreams either, but it's real.

That's when I notice Mom's car parked beside Dad's at the rail of the riding ring. I'd been concentrating so much on Electra that I hadn't heard it pull up, which has to be a major miracle. There's no one in either car so I look around and see three people leaning against the fence watching us. Dad is trying to take some photos of me using his cell phone but it doesn't seem to be going very well. Mom gives me a wave and I can't wave back because I'm holding the reins. And then I see that the third person is Grandpa. Mom must have picked him up at the airport. I didn't think he was coming until next week sometime. He waves at me too and shouts, "Hi there, Pipsqueak! You look great!"

Electra gives her head a toss and the movement ripples right back through me and I grab the front of the saddle.

"Okay, Sylvia, take a deep breath, pay attention, here we go," says Kansas.

After my lesson Grandpa says he wants to take us out for lunch to celebrate and Mom says they should take me home to clean up and change first and Grandpa says Don't be silly, Evie, and Dad says he has some work to do and Mom says, Tony it's a special occasion and I say McDonald's and they all say *No* at once so we go to this fancy place with white table cloths overlooking the ocean not far from where I found the barnacles, which seems fitting somehow.

I'm still so excited I can hardly eat, and I can't stop talking because I have to be sure they noticed everything, like how I stretched my legs down and how I held my hands steady and how I let my back move with the motion of the horse and how I almost fell off but didn't, when Electra stumbled.

The most wonderful thing is that they all look happy and there's not the slightest whiff of guilt in the air and the only talk about money is when Dad and Grandpa argue about who's going to pay the lunch bill and Grandpa wins as usual.

I go home with Dad. Grandpa wants Mom to take him shopping, so they don't get back until later.

I'm showing Dad the video on YouTube of Blue Hors Matine doing her freestyle dressage test at the World Equestrian Games, which is hard because every time I watch it I cry so I can't explain to him exactly what she's doing. But at the end Dad sits there and doesn't say anything for a minute and then he says, "Wow."

Grandpa takes his suitcase to the guest room. He says he's going to unpack, then have a nap. Dad says he needs to review one of the equity funds. Mom has some work to do in the kitchen because Auntie Sally, Taylor and Erika are coming over later for dinner.

I go to the garage to clean and polish my paddock boots, which takes quite a while because to do it properly I have to take out the laces completely and then put them back in again after the polish has dried. I've almost finished when Mom calls me into the house and we go down to my bedroom. Dad and Grandpa are sitting beside each other on my bed.

"I bought you an early birthday present," says Grandpa. He points to a Sears bag leaning against my bedside table.

I open the bag, expecting a wrapped present inside. Instead there's a small plastic footstool.

I hold it in both hands and try to smile. "Thanks, Grandpa." I'm thinking he's so old he really has no idea any more what's an appropriate gift for teenagers. But I don't want to be rude. At least he's trying.

"You're very welcome," says Grandpa. He and Dad sit there on the bed smiling at me and I think maybe I've missed something. I look over at Mom who is smiling too. I smile back at them all.

Grandpa clears his throat. "It's a mounting block."

And my brain freezes up. I'm holding the little stool in front of me, staring at it like it's a live thing, and I know what it's for and I know what I should be doing with it, but I can't move. It's almost like when I was in that dream where Kansas was sitting on my bed holding my foot, I'm that paralyzed. Here I am, about to get exactly what I want in life and I can't take a single step.

Mom pries the footstool out of my fingers and places it at the base of the open door. She takes me by the elbow and guides me over, and somehow I figure out how to put one foot beside the other and stand with my back against the door edge.

"Use a book on her head, Evie," says Grandpa.

"Dad, I know," says Mom. She grabs my Pony Club manual and a pencil from my desk, balances the book on my head and draws a line. I hear the soft snicking sound of the pencil lead on the paint above my ear. I'm afraid to turn around and look. I can see the disappointment on Grandpa's face. Mom sits down beside him.

"Maybe I should have bought a taller stool," he says.

I can't believe it. I take a peek at the door—I'm about a hand short. But that's not the unbelievable part. What I can't believe is how relieved I feel.

"I'm not ready," I tell them.

Mom says, "Sure you are, Honey."

Dad says, "You're a very responsible kid."

Grandpa says, "I've already cashed in the bonds, they matured last month, now the money's sitting in my account waiting to be used."

I stand on the stool and look down on them, perched together on my bed, all trying to look upbeat, all trying to do the right thing. The trouble is, they don't know what the right thing is, and for once I do.

"Kansas says I'm not ready. She says I need to take lessons for a while so that when I do buy my own horse I'll be able to ride it properly. She says any horse that is quiet enough for me to learn on now might not suit me in a year."

Now they all look disappointed.

I look back to the purple mark on the door. "I probably need a year to grow that much anyway. It's perfect, really."

And it is perfect. In a year I'll be good enough at riding to handle a great horse. Grandpa can buy one for me then, as well as a taller footstool, if that's what I need to reach the purple mark. In the meantime, I have a lot to learn. And Mom needs a new car. I know better than to suggest that Grandpa buy her one—I know how Dad will react, whether he understands why or not. But I think I can probably help them work something out. Somehow. It will be an interesting campaign, and marketing is something I am skilled at now. Plus there's something else I plan on learning from Electra, the little boss mare: how to move the herd with the flick of an ear. My next campaign will be so subtle no one will notice a thing.

ACKNOWLEDGEMENTS

I owe a debt of gratitude to many in the creation of this book.

First and foremost, I am thankful to my family and friends for their support and inspiration.

To Hiro Boga at Oolichan Books for, well, everything!

To Isobel Springett for her amazing photography skills.

To Janet, for the barnacles, and Tricia Forrester-Hunter, for her love of dance.

To Richard Ketchen for all that free help with the technical stuff.

Mark Hobby, farrier and tireless source of interesting equine information. Any errors are mine, not his.

My twin, who I have never met, Anna Elvidge, for reading the first draft and responding with such enthusiasm.

Brian Brett for reading an early draft and sending me in the right direction.

Miss Haut and her English classes at G.P. Vanier Secondary School, for listening, laughing at the right bits, and then advising so astutely on the cover.

Dr. Bill Otto, for reviewing medical issues in an early draft. Any errors are mine.

To Kristina and her pals, and Kaela and Alex. Thanks for being girls, and for visiting and letting me see what it's like to be young nowadays.

To two gifted teachers who helped along the way, Jack Hodgins and Matt Hughes.

To my riding pals, who help to keep me in the game, especially Bonnie, Pauline, Natasha and Gina. And my friend Seiko who keeps me on track.

To the horses who have passed through my life: Cloudy, Squirt, Stash, Lucy, Major, Shadow, Cowboy, Blazer and Lollipop.

To Mike, for listening, then listening again . . . and for pretending I wasn't home.

Wonderful. Reads like a cross between Adrian Mole and *The Curious Incident of the Dog in the Night-time.*

—Dr. David Davies,
Child and Adolescent Psychiatrist

I knew Susan rode her horse with intelligence, heart and humour, so I'm not surprised to find that she writes the same way.

—Gina Allan-Belasik, Equine Canada Coach

A smart, modern, witty novel. Curious adolescent equestrian navigates toward her passion. A must family read!"

—John Marton, Ph.D. Psychologist,
and Seiko Marton, Social Worker

Author photo: Terrance Berscheid

Susan Ketchen holds an M.Sc. degree in Marriage and Family Therapy. She lives on a small Vancouver Island hobby farm with her husband, two horses, two cats and a flock of chickens.

Susan is a member of the B.C. Horse Council, the Comox Valley Dressage Club, the Comox Valley Writer's Society and a psychiatry journal club.

She is a monitor with the Wildlife Tree Stewardship Program, giving her an official excuse to spend many hours staring out the window . . . at the eagles perching and nesting at the edge of the property.

She is interested in animal training and teaches her horses to recognize a remarkable number of words, play the piano with their noses, and identify flash cards. She has given up trying to master dressage but still enjoys her riding lessons.

She is inspired by her surroundings, by the animals domesticated and wild, and by the many interesting people in her life. Her favourite places to come up with new ideas are the barn, the pasture, and the shower. She has never received creative inspiration while vacuuming.

www.susanketchen.ca